Lost Ottawa

LOST
OTTAWA

DAVID MᶜGEE

OTTAWA
PRESS AND
PUBLISHING

ottawapressandpublishing.com

ISBN 978-1-988437-03-3 (pbk.)
ISBN 978-1-988437-05-7 (epub)
ISBN 978-1-988437-06-4 (mobi)

Copyright © David McGee 2017

Design and compositon: Magdalene Carson / New Leaf Publication Design

Cataloguing in Publication data available at Library and Archives Canada

The author has made every attempt to locate the sources of photographs.
Should there be errors or omissions, please contact the author
for correction in future printings.

Contents

2013

2014

2015

2016

I would like to thank my wife Anne-Marie Battis. She's the one who suggested that I start Lost Ottawa way back in February of 2013 and put up with me working on it every morning and every night since then. It's got me out of so many kitchen chores!

I would like to give a really big thanks to those unsung heroes who have been toiling away, digitizing photos in archives across the country, including the folks at Library and Archives Canada, and the Canada Science and Technology Museum. A special thanks to the City of Ottawa Archives, where staff worked extra hard in getting photos ready for the publication of this book. Without the work archivists do in making so many historical photos available online, Lost Ottawa would not be possible.

I also want to single out the Ottawa Public Library for the fabulous resources it makes available in the Ottawa Room at the Main Branch.

I would like to thank Magdalene Carson of New Leaf Publication Design for the outstanding work she did in designing this book. Thanks also to Ron Corbett of Ottawa Press and Publishing for his strong belief in regional publishing and his unwavering support of this project.

Finally, I must thank the members of the Lost Ottawa Community. Without their willingness to send photos, post comments, and share their experience, Lost Ottawa just wouldn't be the fabulous conversation that it is.

Introduction

Lost Ottawa began in 2013 as a Facebook community with a simple goal — to find out if people in Ottawa were interested in their history.

This question came up because it seemed to us that little formal history of Ottawa had been written in the past 50 years. True, some excellent books had been produced on various aspects of city life, like movie theatres and city planning, but nothing really major had appeared since John Taylor's *Ottawa: An Illustrated History* of 1983, and Bruce Elliot's *The City Beyond: A History of Nepean* of 1991.

Why was this? Was it because the business model for writing local history was broken and no one could make money at it? Because local history was boring, as so many claim, so no one was interested? Or could it be that people weren't consuming history because they weren't getting the kind of history they wanted, they way they wanted it, on their computers, phones and tablets?

To answer these questions, we decided to conduct a simple experiment by creating a Facebook community page. On this page, we decided we would post historical pictures of the city, together with short descriptions, then ask people to respond and see if they engaged.

Engage they did. Lost Ottawa on Facebook now has approximately 42,000 members. It is the largest historical community in the city, and one of the largest Facebook communities in the Capital Region. Since 2013, we've posted more than 8,000 pictures, each one now viewed by an average of 10,000 people. Our weekly reach — meaning the number of individuals who see our content — regularly exceeds 100,000. These individuals have issued almost one million "likes" of our various posts. Most important, they have left more than 90,000 comments about all things "lost."

What do we mean by "lost?" At one level, we mean things that are gone, like buildings or neighborhoods that just aren't there anymore, or places that have changed beyond all recognition. We also mean things that are "lost in plain sight," maybe still right there, but no longer recognized for what they are. More than anything else, we meant "lost to memory," as in the experience of any place, event, or activity in the city that might have been forgotten, but could be recalled by seeing just a single photograph. Taking all these things together, and "lost" could be just about anything — a house, a store, a concert, a hockey stick, or a burger joint. It's about things like these that the people of Lost Ottawa have written so much.

In this book, we bring the most popular stories from Lost Ottawa together, although what counts as "most popular" on Facebook is a tricky question. You could measure it by the number of likes, the number of shares, or the number of comments. You could measure it by the number of views, or by the number of unique people reached (for which Facebook didn't even have a statistic when we started). Thinking it over, we decided to add the number of likes, shares and comments together to come up with a simple measure for popularity, using the number of comments as a tie-breaker (which almost always gave us the posts with the most views and greatest reach, as well). We used this formula to identify the top posts for each week of every month since we started in 2013. Then we decided to separate the posts into chapters by year. Otherwise, because the Lost Ottawa community keeps growing every year, all the most popular posts would be from 2016.

For each story we've provided the original picture (with just a few exceptions) and a short description. Then comes a selection from the original comments. For the sake of privacy, we've left out last names. Since Facebook posts are often written in a hurry, we've corrected spelling, punctuation, grammar, and sometimes syntax. Sadly, emoticons had to go, along with multiple exclamation marks! We've had to eliminate duplicate comments to save space. And finally, since it's not always easy to know who responded to who on Facebook, we've arranged the comments to create a conversation that flows.

Add it all up and what you get in this book are the most popular stories from Lost Ottawa, as chosen and told by the people themselves. Whether it's riding the streetcars, swimming at the Chateau Laurier, or sipping malted milks at Freiman's Department Store, the stories they tell are always fascinating, sometimes rather opinionated, and frequently hilarious. They are also history. Maybe not your grandfather's history of Great Men (and occasionally women) doing Great Things in the course of Great Events — but history just the same. The history of things that happen to ordinary folks as they live their lives and go about their business. The kind of history that isn't usually written down. The history of common experience. Shared experience.

That's important because shared experience is really the key to community identity, and that's what you get access to in this book. If you're a tourist, you'll read a unique account of Ottawa's people and places. You're sure to discover things about Canada's Capital that your average tourist guide won't tell you. If you're a newcomer to Ottawa, you'll learn more about your fellow citizens and the crazy things they are always talking about. If you grew up here, get ready to relive the experience.

David McGee
Ottawa, July 1, 2017

2013

Our First Post

(CANADA SCIENCE AND TECHNOLOGY MUSEUM, STOWELL COLLECTION)

It was on February 10, 2013 that Lost Ottawa made its first post. It featured a postcard of what was once known as Connaught Plaza — more commonly referred to as "The Plaza" — taken sometime between 1929 and 1938. This postcard nicely complemented our logo of the time, which also showed the Plaza from the air.

Before the War Memorial was built, the Plaza was the centre of Ottawa life. Here you had the city's main post office (on the left), the train station, as well as the biggest and most prestigious hotel. Every one of the city's streetcar lines ran through the Plaza. The line from Hull ran underneath. The top was regularly used for parking, but also for civic events, including rallies, parades, the annual dog derby, the Winter Carnival and more.

In many ways, this first post was a Lost Ottawa classic. It shows a part of the city practically every citizen of Ottawa is familiar with — yet a part of the city that is so different today, with the Plaza, the post office, and the Daly Building gone. That's the sort of post that gets people thinking about the nature of change. Is it for better, or worse?

We received only 12 comments in total, but even our first picture got people talking to each other, and sharing a little Ottawa humour.

Matthew: Seems the road layout has changed significantly since then! Is that Queen Street or Sparks Street in the foreground left to right?

David: The cross street is Sparks, at the junction with the Driveway, bottom centre.

Mike: It's so much nicer than today, Now, Confederation Square is an urban disaster. During peak periods no one can figure it out, which annoys those of us who do know where to go. This looks much more organized.

Andrew: It's not for nothing that it has been known since the '50s as "Confusion Square!"

Gloria: My dad worked at the Chateau Laurier from the time he was 13 until he retired as sous chef around 1980.

Joanne: I did not know your dad was a chef, Gloria. It's funny because my grandfather worked across the street at CN Rail. He was chief engineer and had his office in the front corner of the station.

Reid: It was a totally different place in those days and it's unfortunate that we have not only lost so many buildings, but also the lifeblood that flowed along streets like Bank and Rideau. Core areas across North America, including Ottawa, have suffered more than we can imagine.

Phil: Before you get TOO nostalgic ... back then much of downtown Ottawa would have still been filled with heavy industry. Homes and businesses burned cheap and dirty coal so all exterior surfaces would have been filthy black. Many buildings were firetraps, and abject poverty filled certain quarters of the city ...

Benoit: Yeah, but free parking!

Lucie: I just know I'm going to love this page.

Inside Union Station

February 17, 2013: 49 likes, 27 shares and 27 comments

This magnificent picture was the most popular post of our first week. It shows the waiting hall inside Ottawa's Union Station, circa 1927.

Below the central pillars is the entrance to the famous tunnel under Rideau Street that took you to the Chateau Laurier. Flanking the entrance are two staircases that took you up to the street.

The station was opened in 1912, by Grand Trunk Railway, but the trains stopped coming in 1966, when the tracks along the east side of the Rideau Canal were removed in accordance with the famous/infamous Greber Plan.

The station was then converted into a government conference centre, which, although it is theoretically open to the public, most people have never been in.

Since this post, the station has been renovated again to serve as a temporary home for the Canadian Senate.

Rich: My earliest memory of Union Station was in 1946. I was four years old and my mom took me to meet the troop train carrying my dad home after his four years overseas. All I remember is a sea of khaki uniforms surrounding me at my short height ...

Maureen: My grandmother worked there during the depression. She was the washroom attendant, I believe. I always loved this building and keep meaning to get back inside.

Lorraine: My mom and I used to take the train to Casselman to visit my grandmother. My uncle was a barber at the Chateau, too. I really miss seeing the inside of this building!

Pat: When I was a little fellow I would go with my father to the station to pick up my dad's paycheque. It was a grand building. Took the train a few times back when we had the steam engines. It was so busy back then.

Rita: There was a small office at the top of those monstrous steps. My uncle worked there for Canadian National Railways. My friends and I used to go there to hang out and then go swimming at the Chateau Laurier pool!

Bernice: We used to go swimming in the pool at the Chateau and then through the tunnel to the station, laughing and shouting as we ran through it — it was like an echo chamber.

Marilyn: I also remember the tunnel, swimming at the Chateau for ten or twenty-five cents, then getting the streetcar back to Aylmer.

Ray: You could roll a nickel from the Chateau Laurier to the train station through the tunnel and it would never stop. We used to have races. What a time to remember!

John: My younger brothers and I used to take a five-cent bus down there, especially in winter, to spend Sunday afternoons running around inside where it was warm. I remember the tunnel and I especially remember those lamps above the benches. Great memories!

Jen: I had forgotten how beautiful it is inside. Ottawa doesn't have enough magnificent old architecture that's open to the public.

Chris: It's a shame the building isn't open to the public. I've performed at a couple of events in there and it's beautiful – a gem in the heart of our city that's only used for government functions.

Maggie: This station was beautiful. Such a shame it was closed.

Karen: Our "new" train station on Tremblay is, well, BORING. It's sad to think of all the historic buildings that have been torn down to make way for modern ones. So much could have been done with them.

Terry: Every time I see this, I thank Greber and the politicians of the time who ruined transportation in Ottawa.

Michael: I loved taking the train from this place! I can still hear the echoes in my head!

Chris: Can we please have this building back?

(CANADA SCIENCE AND TECHNOLOGY MUSEUM, CN 28637)

The Great Snow of 1971-72

What could be more Ottawa than a snowstorm? You're looking at me in this photo and the scene was 89 Queensline Drive in the spring of 1972, when the snowbank reached the roof of our split-level home in Graham Park.

Now I am an old hand at such things, but back then my family had just moved from Victoria, British Columbia, where it never snowed during my childhood. We were forced to question our father's sanity.

I posted this photo on the day of a huge blizzard, after escorting a visitor from France around town. She was ecstatic to be in an authentic Canadian snowstorm. To get the full experience, she even helped push a car out of a snowbank.

Penny: I grew up in Ottawa, as did my parents and grandparents, etc. I also question my ancestors' sanity. Why didn't they keep going until they found a valley with more hospitable winters? Did the sleigh runners get frozen to the river? Did a cloud of black flies overwhelm them? Did they succumb to heat stroke in July?

Anne: This was the winter we were able to just step onto the roof of our garage and build a snow fort. I have never seen that much snow since.

Allan: I remember the snowbanks topping out that winter at our second story windows in Leslie Park. They were so tall that we made toboggan runs.

Max: I remember the tunnels we used to dig into the snowbanks. It's so amazing that we survived our youth!

Robert: I don't think it was amazing, Max ... I think we were a lot more alert about our surroundings and more or less knew the hazards involved ... and that's what made it all the more exciting.

Grant: I lived on this street — it was so fun building snow forts, tunneling through the banks, and throwing snowballs. Try that nowadays.

Lee-Ann: I remember these snowfalls as a kid. You still had to go to school. There was no such thing as a "snow day." But those huge snowbanks sure made for great snow forts ... I'm guessing kids nowadays don't know how to build snow forts.

Barb: No school buses and no "snow days" for us back then. We would leave a little earlier in the winter because it took so long to climb up and down the snowbanks. We never walked on the road or sidewalk, because it was much more fun to climb the snowbank and walk on the top. We made a lot of money shoveling driveways, too, because there was no such thing as a snowblower.

Brian: I lived in Richmond that year. You could not even see the school bus, there was so much snow.

Karin: I remember living in Rockcliffe and skating all over the base when the freezing rain turned the streets into thick ice. My parents kept the survival certificate!

Barb: These are the winters I remember as a kid. Not the wimpy winters we get now ... mind you now that I'm older I sure appreciate these wimpy winters.

Jen: I honestly wondered if I had only imagined how high the snow was. Or maybe my view was distorted by the fact I was only 7 years old!

Pat: I remember it all well — it's the main reason I now live in Victoria, BC, where today it is 9 degrees (that is +9), raining, and the annual blossom count is on.

(LOST OTTAWA)

7

Eaton's in Bayshore

March 29, 2013: 71 likes, 22 shares, and 42 comments

When the Bayshore Shopping Centre opened on August 8, 1973, it had four anchor stores — the Bay on the west; Miracle Mart and Steinberg's in the middle; and Eaton's on the east.

Most of the mall was two storeys high, but Eaton's was three storeys, so this entrance was on top of the original parking structure.

Eaton's went out of business in 1999. The Bay is the only one of the original anchor stores left. Funny, at the time I always thought The Bay would be the first to go.

Kimberley: Gosh, I remember this entrance.

Ann: I remember my dad and I standing on the second level and you could feel it vibrating!

Lee: I worked at this Eaton's for many years. The metal doors on the right were the employee entrance.

(ARCHIVES OF ONTARIO I0016059.JPG)

Carol: I used to go dirt biking on the property, before they built the shopping centre.

Marnie: I remember when this shopping centre was only a Steinberg's and a Royal Bank, then it became this beautiful place where we loved to shop.

Ron: I used to clean the Royal Bank at the strip plaza before it became Bayshore.

Karin: Does anyone remember the very large fountain on the lower level? The "food court" was one or two little refreshment stands on the second floor where Charm Jewelers now stands.

Olivia: I think I fell into that fountain when I was a kid while trying to get a closer look!

Sabina: I remember the fountain! I used to giggle at it as a child since it had naked people!

James: Out in the mall, the two Pik-Niks were main locations for getting food, prior to the food court and the third floor being added in the mid-'80s.

Karen: I used to work at the Pik Nik! It was owned by Steinberg's.

Trevor: Steinberg's. There's a name that's been lost for more than a few years.

Barbara: OMG! I used to do my groceries at Steinberg's when we lived on Arnold Drive.

Janine: I loved the elaborate conveyor belt system Steinberg's had for the grocery pick-up. That was cool.

Rick: Nice! My brother and I both worked at Steinberg's, starting there in 1974. I still work in the industry at Sobeys. We were just leaving the mall, when robbers were confronted by two Nepean policemen and they had that shoot-out there.

Alma: I worked at Dalmy's years ago and lived in the neighbourhood when it was safe. Loved working those hours until 10 p.m. — NOT!

Max: One day when I was working at Bayshore, the regular Santa called in sick, so I had to fill in. I must have weighed all of 135 lbs. Skinny as a rake. The pillows didn't fool those nasty kids and the elves were mean. That was a rough few hours! You couldn't pay me enough to do it again.

Theresa: I used to work at the information desk that was in between the up and down escalators. Spent my time telling people where to go ...

Christopher: I worked at the historic "HMV" where they sold these round music-playing discs that you had to put into a player and change by hand. Let's all take a moment to appreciate how old we are.

The Chickulator
at Science and Tech

April 11, 2013: 227 likes, 50 shares and 78 comments

The chick incubator was one of the most beloved attractions at the Science and Technology Museum on St. Laurent Boulevard, an excellent example of what made Science and Tech the most popular museum in Ottawa in the '60s and '70s.

Housed in a cabinet that looked like a flying saucer (but which was originally intended to suggest a fried egg) the "Chickulator" was simple in concept, but powerful in action. Eggs were heated under the dome. The chicks hatched. Kids climbed right on top, learning where food came from by watching only inches away.

On the Science and Tech Museum floor since at least 1968, the incubator was moved to the Agriculture Museum at the Experimental Farm in the late '90s, and later disappeared.

Patrick: What? The chicks are gone? WHO is responsible?

Shauna: That was my favourite part!

Laura: My kids loved, loved, loved the hatchery when I brought them to the "touching things" museum.

Blaine: Cycled four kids through that brilliant exhibit. Low tech and high fascination. Shame it's gone.

Steve: I had totally forgotten about this, but I remember the days when the crazy kitchen was right near the main entrance. It was one of the first things you walked through, once you passed the big rotating model of Earth.

Carrie: I loved the hatchery as a kid, and was also enthralled with the world globe when you first walked in. I remember thinking the trains were the biggest things I'd ever seen. Love that museum!

Chantal: The chicks in that spaceship incubator, and the crazy kitchen (as well as the trains and cars) — those were the highlights when I was a kid in the '70s.

Douglas: My son and I went about every other weekend to watch and "wow" at this display. The crazy kitchen, steam trains, and the swirling steel ball exhibits were our favourites.

Adam: The hatchery was one of my faves. With a scientist for a dad, you can imagine we visited at least six times a year, every year. Between the chicks, the reaction-time self-tester, the trains and the crazy kitchen experience — what more could you want, right?

Lana: I still remember the way it felt to climb up on the incubator and try not to slide off while gazing in. It was slippery, and you had to continually hold onto the edge of the hot glass to be able to see. Can you imagine what those chicks' first thoughts were when they came out of the eggs? Maybe, "Ahhh! Put me back in!"

Ted: I remember this sooo well — and here is a true story. When I was little I managed to climb on top of it. I gazed down into it and said "Look dad, chicken nuggets!"

Andrea: I remember you doing that! Or at least, in all my years working at the museum, there was only one kid who ever did it, so it must have been you. You horrified a whole group of parents who couldn't clap their hands over their kids' ears fast enough.

Peter: I loved it … but it actually turned me off eating eggs for years and years.

Helen: It looks like a flying saucer. I wonder what happened to the chicks, but maybe I don't want to know …

11

Ogilvy's Department Store

May 11, 2013: 150 likes, 24 shares and 58 comments

Saturday Shopping: featuring an Ogilvy's bag from the much-loved department store, which was famous for its tartan boxes and bags.

It was tartan because Charles Ogilvy was a Scottish immigrant who opened his first store at 92 Rideau Street in 1887. The business moved down Rideau to the corner of Waller and continued to grow for nearly a century, finally going out of business in 1992.

The beautiful Ogilvy's facade was recently saved and re-incorporated into a new building. Looks good!

Ken: I used to love how they had a piper open the store on the first morning of their annual fall sale.

(SHARED BY KEN CLAVETTE)

Kathy: I miss the Robbie Burns celebration in the cafeteria, when the Ogilvy pipe band would play in the haggis, and someone from the Burns Society would recite the Ode to the Haggis, and everyone got a free piece.

Tina: My grandmother worked at Charles Ogilvy's. She was the pretty elevator girl, in uniform and everything! Does anyone remember the old fashioned elevator? It was the coolest thing. Well, that and the malts!

Marcel: I worked at Robert Simpsons on Sparks Street Mall. It was the same type of store and they had the old elevators, with all young women working them.

Lee: I remember Ogilvy's was the first company that had the escalators that were flat, so strollers and wheelchairs could use them.

Teresa: I remember those bags!

Heather: Ogilvy's always had the best shoes in town, so those bags often contained beautiful shoes.

Patricia: The highlight of the new school year was to shop at Ogilvy's for new shoes!

Eva: I have one of these bags in my bathroom closet. It holds my mom's hair curlers. Not used in a long time!

Isabel: Whenever my mum wanted to buy us something "special" to wear, it came from Ogilvy's.

Helen: I still have the TV stand I bought there ... and somehow rolled home to my apartment.

Pau: I remember several years of birthday and Christmas presents (e.g. shirts) coming in boxes with the tartan stripe down one side.

Mark: My mother worked there for years and I worked there when I was at University, in housewares. People would often buy a cheap gift, then ask for one of those smart boxes. I wonder how many bits of tat from Woolworth's ended up at a wedding in a huge blue Ogilvy's box?

Gayle: My mother worked at the Rideau Street store and later at Billings Bridge. She worked in the "foundation department," where you were actually measured and fitted!

Barry: Ogilvy's, in Ottawa, was privately owned by the store employees and the Hyndman family of Ottawa and it was truly a store that treated its employees with the greatest of dignity. Each year there was a stock offering and the employees could buy shares. Those that weren't bought were offered to those who wanted them. Very few ever complained about working there and it was a real family atmosphere. The clientele were treated with the best service. City politics and cheap retail competition was the eventual end of the Ogilvy's store.

Charles: It's a shame it was ever sold to Robinson's, which then ran it into the ground, killing one of the longest-surviving department stores in Ottawa. Then look what happened to Robinson's. KARMA ...

Merrill: Ogilvy's is the first store my aunt would hit with me (when we went shopping.) Than it was Freiman's for a chocolate malt!

Barry: Those basement malts were the greatest!

Rolande: The malts! Loved those. Didn't they have those in the basement of The Bay on Rideau? And wasn't the Bay a Freiman's before that?

Heather: Yes, it used to be called Freiman's. The malts were in the basement ... and they were to die for.

The Towers Store on Cyrville

May 15, 2013: 107 likes, 59 shares and 70 comments

(LIBRARY AND ARCHIVES CANADA 4068557)

Here's the Towers department store in December 1964, two years after it opened at 1250 Cyrville Road in the east end.

"At Towers everything connects – the last day of one sale is the first day of the next," was the Towers jingle. Maybe not so catchy?

In 1990, Towers went out of business, and was taken over by Zellers, but people remember the original store with great fondness.

Adele: I learned to drive in this parking lot on Sundays, when the store was closed. I also remember shopping there with my parents for living room furniture that lasted forever, and I still have Christmas decorations bought there as a newlywed. When I was pregnant with my second child, I would bring my son to ride the turtle in the entrance while we enjoyed the air conditioning. Good times!

Kelly: One day, one of their trinket machines wasn't working properly when I put in money. I forget how much it was — but the machine emptied! I had to scoop up my dress and use it to hold them all, there were so many. What a great day that was!

Kim: I used to play Miss Packman and Popeye at Towers.

Mark: Hey, Kim. That's Pacman.

Kim: Oops! Mark you're right ... and it was "Ms. Pacman."

Ben: I used to go to Towers near Cyrville road with my mother all the time. I remember they had a water fountain at the entrance and the water was ice cold! I loved it! I would fill my bladder when we arrived, empty it and refill it again on the way out!

Trish: I used to love that store, and the snack bar was yummy. I especially loved the corn dogs.

Cathy: Loved the hot dogs on a stick.

Lee: I had family and friends who worked at Towers. I really miss the older, German lady named Krista who worked in the cafeteria.

Charlotte: A friend of mine was the long-time manager and they brought in the first computerized retail system in the city. That computer took up a lot of space!

Gilles: I worked there as a cashier for my first job. Didn't last long. You needed to know what to and what not to charge tax on. Some people got a tax-free day ... others, not so lucky!

Max: This store reminds me of Shoppers City, but I can't remember which plaza had which stores.

Anthony: JDS bought this building when Zellers moved to the old Kmart location on St. Laurent. It is now a DND facility.

Francine: Shoppers City East was off Blair Rd.

Nata: Shoppers City East was at Blair and Ogilvie and had a Freimart and an IGA and later a Loblaw's and a Bay Home Store. Now it has a Beer Store, LCBO, Shoppers Drug Mart, Dollarama, and a Giant Tiger. Shoppers City West at Baseline and Woodroffe had a Freimart and an IGA, and later a Loblaw's and something else, all torn down for the new plaza. Towers was on Cyrville, and paired with a Loblaw's, and later became a Zellers. Still later, the building was renovated to house part of JDS Uniphase, which went out of business before the company could move in.

Susan: Shoppers City West was to die for when I was a kid. I had forgotten about it. Friday night shopping with the family, when I was less than six-years old. We got big bags of popcorn.

Roy: The little snack bar in Shoppers City West certainly had hot dogs to die for. Toasted flat buns. Awesome.

Barb: Oh sure, you had to remind me about those hot dogs. They were good.

Wagon Ride on the Edge of Town

May 24, 2013: 107 likes, 33 shares and 35 comments

(SHARED BY MARCIA MORDFIELD)

A local farmer takes neighborhood kids for a wagon ride along Innes Road, near Stonehenge Crescent, in the '80s.

At the time, Innes at Blair was the edge of the city and the new neighborhoods were still bordered by farmland. One kindly farmer used to hook up his horse and wagon and take the kids for free rides around the area. The Apple Saddlery on Innes is a reminder of those days.

Janet: I used to love going on those wagon rides. That's my house in the background.

Marion: I forgot what the houses looked like when we moved in.

Mathieu: Freaky. I grew up on the corner of Stonehenge and Whittaker and may actually BE in that picture.

Robert: I might be in that picture, too.

Lynn: I think I actually am on that wagon.

Karin: I think the farmer's name was Doug Woodburn. His family originally owned most of the land in that area. Those are most likely his horses in the pic.

Marcia: Karin is right, the farm belonged to Doug Woodburn and we also got to feed the horses on his farm. I remember one called Rusty.

Catherine: Wow! I rode with Mr. Woodburn on that wagon along with Andrea and Daniel. It was always fun. Doug is still there running the farm and I wave at him all the time.

Robert: I went to school with Kim Woodburn, and I recall going for a sleigh ride with our school at her father's farm. It would have been sometime around 1980.

Kevin: Kim, look familiar?

Kim: The horses' names were Willard and Ugly Doug. We called him Ugg for short.

Maureen: I remember riding Mr. Woodburn's horses along the NCC parkway in the '70s — and being chased off by the RCMP.

Deb: Mr. Woodburn had a pony named Pokie, and he used to let my son and I go into the barn to see the animals. Once in a while he'd give us a few fresh eggs.

Keith: I lived near there for a year in '76, when I was 8. I remember going to the farm all the time and sneaking into the barn. I remember the farmer giving me fresh cut cucumbers with salt.

Vicki: I think that farm was still active when I moved to the area in 1989. I remember a milk truck coming to collect the milk in the mornings when I was waiting for the bus on Innes Road.

Elias: I live on Meadowvale Lane off Stonehenge, across the street from the farm. As of last summer, the horses and cows were in the fenced-in field. You could also hear the rooster crowing in the morning.

Stephanie: I lived on Stonehenge in 1985, when what is now the Apple Saddlery used to be called the Gloucester Farmers Market and it was the only store for miles.

Sarah: We used to shop for meat every week at the Gloucester Farmers Market. Doug is still around the yard beside the Apple Saddlery, by the way. It's now a very nice store run by Doug's wife, Sherry.

Ruthanne: I live just off Stonehenge now, across from the field by the Apple Saddlery. There haven't been any critters in the field since the fall. When we moved here in 2000, there was still a barn and a grain silo on the other side of Innes. Now there is a Rona and McDonald's. Sigh.

Demise of the Dairy Queen Sign at St. Laurent and Hemlock

May 31, 2013: 175 likes, 160 shares and 211 comments

Sometimes you can be dumb but lucky. It was certainly dumb luck that helped me get this picture of an old neon sign being hauled away from the Dairy Queen at Hemlock and St. Laurent.

I was taking a colleague to lunch, so I decided not to bother bringing a camera, but as we pulled into the parking lot I saw the sign on the trailer. It was so Old School and so beautiful, I assumed it was just being taken away for repair. I took a photo with my phone.

A few days later, the Ottawa Citizen reported that the sign had been removed and destroyed on orders of DQ head office, against the wishes of the storeowners. Good thing I had my phone!

The sign dated from 1958 when the DQ first opened in Manor Park. A lot of people were rather upset about its disappearance.

Rae: Nooooooo ...

Sébastien: NOOOOOOO!!

Angela: NOOOOOOOOOOOOOOO. NO NO NO NO NO NO NO!

Inger: That sign meant summer for a lot of Ottawans.

Robert: So sad ... this sign was a landmark in the east end.

(LOST OTTAWA)

Jason: Morons.

Don: Corporate jerks!

Susan: Are they nuts? They have no understanding how old is new again. Retro is cool and it is very sad to hear the sign is being demolished.

Michel: That is sad! I grew up standing in line at that DQ and now take my kids. I guess they'll be sad too, when they are my age and they pull down the new sign to destroy it.

Lynne: My dad and I used to go to that DQ every Saturday afternoon on the way to my uncle's cottage. We'd share a banana split and each have the small bottles of Orange Crush. I am disappointed.

Dave: My friends and I would bike there all the time for ice cream. It was literally a sign that it was summertime. Really sad to see it go.

Beverley: It used to taste soooo good. On a hot summer eve there would be lineups to get served!

Lisa: Every time dad said on a Sunday night, "let's go for a drive" ... we always knew the translation was: "let's go to DQ!"

Kathryne: My friend and I walked there every Sunday for a milk shake ... mine was peppermint!

Kristina: My parents would take me there after a soccer game.... Go Manor Park Mighty Mites! Um ... I think I gave away my age with that one!

John: This was my local DQ when I lived on Braemar Ave. I remember one of my baseball teammates broke that sign with his baseball while celebrating one of our (very) rare Little League wins in Manor Park.

Mona: I remember it well. My brother Chris used to work there in the summer, and I guess he wore sandals at work because, when he came home late at night, our dog Nicky would lick his toes clean.

Gib: As a teenager I worked in that DQ for several summers. One week I worked 93 hours! My pay was 50-cents per hour and I bought my first car with the proceeds. I have so many memories of that DQ. The training I got stayed with me for a lifetime.

Mark: My sis worked there too! They had to let her go for giving out too many extra swirls on your cone. But wreck the sign? Doesn't make sense!

Christine: They call it progress. How sad.

Gord: Sometimes the path of progress is leaving things as they are.

Steven: Progress sucks.

Christina: My childhood is now officially over.

Fred: A moment of silence.

Queen Elizabeth Cuts a Cake

July 1, 2013: 176 likes, 100 shares and 30 comments

Canada Day in 1967 was a big deal. Even Queen Elizabeth II came to the party on Parliament Hill to cut the cake for Canada's 100th birthday.

What a small knife for such a large cake. There still seems to be a question about how much of the cake was real ...

Barb: I will never forget 1967. My family spent the whole day downtown. Later in the day, university students combined with everyday people and did a conga line all around the driveway in front of the Parliament buildings. What a sight that was. I asked mom if we could join and she said no. She didn't want to lose any of us. I was only seven years old. What a day!

Joyce: I was there and remember that day — in my red polka dot dress.

Marlene: I remember that day so well. It was my first time on the Hill for the celebrations, which I continued to do until the '90s. Local step-dancer Donnie Gilchrist and his troupe performed all day in the blaring heat!

Dave: My group, The Five D, performed for Queen Elizabeth and Prince Philip that day on the steps in front of the Centre Block.

Debbie: My brother Peter and I were there, right up front. What an exciting Centennial summer that was!

Peter: I remember the cake had silver dollars inserted, or rather baked in. More important, as Prince Phillip left the stage he patted little Debbie (my sister) on top of her red curly head. How cute! Now everyone knows.

Liz: Just before the cake was cut, a little boy crawled under the fence and walked right up to the royal couple and said, "Hi Queen. Hi Duke." He was a kindergarten student at Hopewell at the time. Maybe he reads Lost Ottawa.

Sue: I remember watching Queen Elizabeth cut the cake and we all had a piece.

Gayle: My family and I were on the Hill and enjoyed a piece!

Liz: There were little cake slices for everyone (but not all from the big cake.)

Jane: I wonder who made the cake? Morrison Lamothe Bakery, perhaps?

Vicki: And was it all real cake, or something fake as well?

John: The cake was made by Morrison Lamothe, and it was made of plywood covered in real icing. There was a small section where real cake was inserted, and that is what the Queen is cutting. The knife she used to cut the cake was the same one used by her father to cut his birthday cake in 1939. Grete Hale has the knife mounted in her dining room today.

Lisa: And here was me, thinking that your Canadian grass and trees are bigger than our English ones, and you have ginormous cakes too!

Rob: Jean Piggott (of the Morrison Lamothe family and a former Ottawa politician) told a great story of the cake and how it was delivered to Parliament Hill. It was too large to fit through the gate, so last minute work was required to get it through.

Joyce: I knew it would be Morrison Lamothe. They delivered bread and cupcakes on the farm when I was a kid.

(LIBRARY AND ARCHIVES CANADA 3408586)

Anthony: I lived two blocks away from the bakery (Lees Avenue). I used to go with my mom to purchase day-old bread or the Vachon cakes like Joe Louis, and the Half-Moon.

Cynthia: Surprising she is showing her bare arms. Must have been a hot, muggy day in Ottawa!

Brent: The Queen got pipes!

Judy: Lovely photo. Does she ever let go of her purse?

Last Days of the Capitol Theatre

July 3, 2013: 150 likes, 88 shares and 70 comments

The Capitol Theatre opened on the southwest corner of Queen and Bank in 1924. It closed in 1970, amid an ugly wave of "urban renewal" that brought destruction not only to Bank Street but to areas like Lowertown and Rideau Street as well.

The outside of the theatre wasn't much to look at. The inside, however, was fabulous. It had a "marble" staircase, an amazing chandelier and a huge auditorium, resplendent with classical moldings, putti, and lush velvet drapes. Being there made you feel like a million bucks.

But the Capitol was much more than a movie palace. It had a stage big enough for all kind of performances, from ballet to symphony, country to rock. Many people saw their first live performances at the Capital. The theatre was also home to endless graduations, club meetings and safety patrol jamborees.

All this made the Capitol Theatre a central node in the city's social life. So it's not surprising how upset people were when it was demolished.

Soula: A memorable place for me. My first date with my husband was at the Capitol, some 53 years ago.

Cheryl: My parents met at the Capitol in the early '40s.

Maria: I remember the staircase and the chandelier.

Barb: I felt like I was going to something special every time I walked up that beautiful staircase. Those were the days when being taken to a movie made you dress up a little more.

(ELIZABETH G. AMEY, SHARED BY BRIAN STANTS)

Sandra: The staircase inside the theatre was incredible. I remember I cried the day they tore it down.

Manos: What a special place, with that lobby, the circular stairs, the huge chandelier. I saw the Bolshoi Ballet there, as well as Nana Mouskouri, Harry Belafonte, Barbara Streisand, Johnny Mathis, Maurice Chevalier, Petula Clark, and Charles Aznavour – with Prime Minister Pierre Elliot Trudeau waiting in line to buy a drink.

Rose: Saw Cream at the Capitol in '67. It was great.

Graeme: My mother-in-law saw the Jimi Hendrix Experience there in '68!

Heather: Don't forget that Hendrix opened for the Monkees, and was booed by the Monkees fans!

Heather: Saw my first rock concert at the Capitol – The Who! It was the perfect, intimate, gaudy and beautiful venue for it.

Stacey: My grandmother worked at the Capitol, so when my mom got kicked out of kindergarten she would go to work with my grandmother there. She could have all the free popcorn she wanted, but only one chocolate bar a day. Popcorn is still her favorite snack!

Dennis: In Grade 7 and 8, Mrs. Evelyn Pook taught us English at Pinecrest Public School (1967-1969). She began by playing an LP vinyl recording of Hamlet, while we read along in our books. Then she assigned roles, and we acted out the story by reading from the books. Then she loaded us onto a bus and took us to the Capitol Theatre to see Hamlet acted live on stage by professionals. Thank you, Mrs. Pook. Thank you, Capitol Theatre!

Antoni: Another travesty. Alas, it's just a matter of time before the Chateau Laurier is torn down for a condo or the canal filled in. But think of the bright side – if these buildings hadn't been torn down, there'd be no need for Lost Ottawa!

(ELIZABETH G. AMEY, SHARED BY BRIAN STANTS)

Commuting on Scott Street

July 8, 2013: 245 likes, 94 shares and 40 comments

(SHARED BY ANDREW MAFFRE)

It's not that often that a diesel locomotive pulls up beside you at a red light! Here's one on Scott Street, circa 1976, and about to head west on the Canadian Pacific tracks near there.

This picture was shared by Andrew Maffre, who observed that Canadian Pacific passenger trains using that track departed from Union Station, passed under the Chateau Laurier, crossed the Alexandra Bridge to Hull, then crossed back over the Prince of Wales Bridge, before heading west along Scott Street to parts beyond.

This locomotive is pulling a freight train on a spur line that crossed Scott to reach the CP tracks (which later turned into the Transitway for buses, and will soon be train tracks again.) The spur line served the Beach Foundry.

Kathy: I'm wondering why there's a guy crossing the intersection when there's a train coming straight at him!?

Ted: Those old, urban at-grade crossings used to be so commonplace, and now seem so outlandish.

Mihal: Wow. I walk through that intersection daily. Crazy to think there used to be tracks. It's so busy with busses and cars these days the train would never get through!

Stephen: I grew up right near there, so seeing this puts a smile on my face. I can remember the gas station and the small liquor store just up Holland. Decades later ... here I am living at Holland Cross.

Matthew: Used to kick soccer balls back and forth over slow moving trains at Ross and Scott by Tunney's Pasture.

Tino: If I'm not mistaken this train has just left the HUGE Beach Foundry that is now Holland Cross. I lived about 4 blocks west of here and remember getting up to look out the window at night when the train puttered by Tunney's.

Gilles: Right, the train is coming from a spur siding, where it had dropped off or picked up boxcars at the foundry, which was between Holland and Parkdale avenues. So the train is actually northbound across Scott St. I believe the bus is the 52 Carlingwood, and is in the left lane waiting to turn on Holland towards Wellington.

Tino: Definitely Holland. The guy standing is on the east side.

Patrick: I suspect that the construction equipment is there to start ripping up the tracks after that train had finished its work. That's likely why the picture was taken ... the last train to Beach Foundry.

Beverley: You could be right!

Mike: Pull out the tracks in the '70s and put them back in 2013-2018. Planning in Ottawa at its best.

Beverley: I'm pretty sure the equipment shown on the left is the start of construction of the Coates Building in Tunney's. I started working in Tunney's in late 1970 and that building wasn't completed at the time.

David: OC Transpo didn't start painting the buses red and white until very late in 1973 and early '74.

Ryan: If the construction on the left side of the photo is for the R.H. Coates building, than this would be '76 or earlier.

Andre: The beige/wood panel wagon at the lights is a Dodge Aspen/ Plymouth Volare — which began production in 1976. So it's after that.

Thomas: Okay, but who has the right of way?

Patrick: In those days trains had the right of way ... everyone else stopped to let the train through ... well, after the light turned red.

At the Back of the Bus

July 9, 2013: 195 likes, 41 shares, 67 comments

This is the inside of one of the buses used by the Ottawa Transportation Commission in 1959, when the OTC adopted an all-bus strategy and the streetcars were abandoned.

I recall these buses rattled like hell. They always made me sick if it took more than half-an-hour to get anywhere.

It was 45 minutes to Carleton University from our house.

Judy: I remember how much they rattled and that they were a kind of green/brown outside. I recall when the fare went up to 15 cents. You gave the driver a quarter and asked for change, then stuck your dime and nickel in the fare box. A lot of the bus stops were just street poles with OTC painted on them. I often took the number 5.

Micheline: They had coin holders to provide change if you needed it to pay your fare.

Heather: I think these had diesel engines, which greatly contributed to the smell, noise and sick feeling. The engine was in the back and constantly blew hot fumes. They were a misery on a hot day.

Vince: The 41 bus was one of the worst. So many turns! Plus, if you sat near the back the diesel fumes made you sick. When I went to Algonquin College I started every day with a headache.

Isabel: Bus trips always made me sick ... and I was only taking the bus from Bank and Foxbar (way out in the country at that time) to the Mayfair Theatre. Plus, there was always the sickening smell of stale cigars in the bus shelter at Bank and Grove.

Louise: And don't forget people were also allowed to smoke on the bus itself.

Pat: Right up to the early '70s, I think.

Louise: We loved these buses. They were noisy, yes, but they gave you a hell of a ride. We loved it when the bus jumped over the train tracks in Overbrook. We'd fall off our seat and laugh like crazy. Great times.

Dorothy: As kids, we would go right to the back seat because that provided the most bounces! We called them the "bumpity buses!"

Hélène: My uncle Simon ruined his back, driving those buses for so long he eventually had to have some of his vertebrae fused.

Gary: I remember riding these buses. You used to hurry so you could get one of the single seats.

Lorie: As a kid in the '60s, I used to ride the 52 downtown from Carlingwood. Loved scoring a single seat!

Deb: When I was about four, my mom and I would go to my dad's office on payday to get cash for the groceries. My favourite place to sit was on the single seats along the driver's side. I always called them the "lonely seats."

Kathy: When I rode buses as a kid, you pulled the cord for your stop. It would buzz rather than ding. The seats were a lot more comfy than the current molded rocks.

Francine: I took these buses so often to go downtown to shop at Freiman's. The number 2 from Vanier!

Karen: I remember being "all dressed up" on a bus like this with nanny and a pile of shopping bags!

Jan: I'm picturing a bygone era, in which my mom and me would take the 50 (now 16) downtown and she would laugh and tell me about streetcars and how Westboro was out in the boonies when she was a kid, and the area from Dovercourt to Carling was a swamp.

Tino: I remember coming home on the 51 to Tunney's Pasture from the Byward Market with my mom ... and two live chickens in a sack!

(LOST OTTAWA)

Goodbye Ottawa Streetcar

July 12, 2013: 100 likes, 51 shares and 19 comments

GOOD BYE OTTAWA. To THE JUNK YARD

(CANADA SCIENCE AND TECHNOLOGY MUSEUM MAT-01028)

The Ottawa Transportation Commission (OTC) took over the Ottawa Electric Railway (OER) in 1950, following a proposed OER fare increase that led to a referendum in 1948 that saw city residents vote overwhelmingly for public ownership.

Unfortunately, pubic ownership did not solve the transportation problems. One was that OER had not been able to modernize its fleet during WWII. Massive capital investment was needed, but the OTC didn't have the money to replace the aging streetcars, nor extend the streetcar tracks.

Following a consultant's report, the OTC went for an all-bus solution in 1959. The photo above shows OTC streetcar 869 on its way to the scrapyard in 1956.

Skip: I went to the parade where all the old streetcars were draped in black, with slogans like this one, just before they went for scrap.

Bob: I believe the photo was taken on the Britannia Line, where the cars were lined up for the scrapper to remove. Circa 1958 or 1959, after abandonment of this line.

Garry: I lived in Britannia Beach and remember seeing these big whales coming down the street!

Trevor: There's a group of volunteers working to restore 696, which ran on the Britannia line.

Tim: Rumour has it the destruction of the streetcars was a conspiracy of the automobile companies, namely GM. Wondering if this was an influence in Ottawa.

Barb: It was pressure from the automotive industry and the oil companies to convert people to automobiles. So sad that Ottawa was a victim, because Toronto still has its streetcars. What a loss. I remember my mom and two oldest sisters telling me how they used to ride it, but I only remember walking on the leftover rails on Sparks Street, before they tore them up, and my mom saying, "Get off of there! You're going to break a bone!"

David: It's a shame Ottawa lost its streetcars, but only Toronto, Montreal and Vancouver were able to upgrade their streetcar fleets before WWII. When Canada entered the war in 1939, Canadian streetcar production was halted. While it is true that GM and other auto-related firms were guilty of American anti-trust law by taking over U.S. transit systems after the war, streetcars were already on the wane in many Canadian cities. Ottawa never upgraded their fleet after the 1920s. Its infrastructure was badly dated (the devil strip, for example, was too narrow for newer cars). Gasoline rationing, full employment and the shortage of automobiles during WWII extended the lives of the streetcars, but by the late '40s the writing was on the wall.

Steve: Big mistake! Toronto was also lobbied to get rid of its streetcars. Good thing the city didn't listen!

Denis: Took Ottawa 50 years to realize the mistake it made by ending the streetcars. Two billion dollars later and all we get is one line.

Rick: It's amazing to think that in another 50 years the city will still be paying for LRT and you still won't be able to ride it to the airport. Such a shame.

Christine: The city of Ottawa was wrong to take the tracks out. So much money could have been saved and now we are paying billions to put them back. Someone needs to fire all those people and get new people who know what they are doing.

Garry: I would ride these with my "girlfriend" in 1953, all the way from Gladstone to the Andrew Fleck day care center on King Edward. With our moms watching we both would sing, "once I had a secret love," at the top of our lungs! Man that was a magical, beautiful time to be alive!

Big Bud's on Bank Street

(SHARED BY MICHAEL PERRON)

Big Bud's was a cut-price store on Bank Street, near Gladstone. It sold just about everything you can think of — really cheap.

Everyone agrees, however, that the key to the Big Bud experience was Big Bud himself.

He was a character of the kind they don't seem to make anymore, and that might be why this picture of the storefront at Bud's, taken just after it closed, was one of the top three posts of our first year.

Jeanette: Strange memory, but didn't Bud yell a lot at customers?

Lee: Yes, he did.

Tanis: Yes. And at the staff, too.

Michael: That guy was a jerk. Always yelling at his employees.

Gisele: Yep ... I remember that as well!

John: I recall that he wasn't the most pleasant guy.

Francine: In the '80s, I worked at the Women's Credit Union on the corner of Bank and Gloucester. On pay day we all ran to Big Bud's to buy our necessities. I remember Mr. Bud yelling at his employees, shamefully. I always wanted to give him a piece of my mind ... but always chickened out.

Anne: I remember a big guy standing at the cash, directing everyone. Including his customers.

Marnie: He was rude and foul-mouthed and totally unapologetic about it. He used to berate customers, but it was always a comedy show in Big Bud's. Some shoppers would be so insulted they would leave their purchases and storm out of the store, but he always left a big tip when he came to my restaurant — although he did make some of the other girls cry because of his insults.

Marlene: Loved Big Bud's and Bud himself. What a character! With a mouth like his, I wonder why he wasn't sued! It was great fun going in there. He was one of "The Good Guys!"

Judy: Loved that store. He sold the largest bottles of Egg Shampoo and Cream Rinse. And closed on Mondays!

Seamus: Wow! I remember those HUGE bottles of egg shampoo! What a memory blast!

Angela: I used to buy huge blocks of pure, olive oil soap — $1.00 each.

Shirley: I use to buy smokes there. Cheapest place in town.

Venda: The cheapest toilet provisions for poor students, and then some food ... dating myself!

Kevin: Best place to buy cheap pop on hot summer days.

Brett: Still use the salt-and-pepper shakers I bought there. The ashtrays are gone.

Carya: I loved going there when I was little. I still have a Barbie lunch box I bought there ...

Susan: I loved Big Bud's. Got an OXO salad spinner there, at half the cost of the big stores (my mother was having dental surgery that day and to keep my mind off her pain I went to Big Bud's.) I still have it and used it tonight. MEMORIES.

Cindy: I loved hearing Bud yell across the store for a floor person to help out a shopper — and the packers calling to the cashier "99 non, 1.29 non" to indicate a taxable item or not.

Francine: I shopped there in my 20s. You had to be quick at the checkout with your bags, or they would be throwing you out the door! I also remember them yelling their prices at the cash, 99 non, 1.99 non ...

Nathalie: Big Bud was a hoot — most of the time. Once I remember being behind a gent who was buying some Brylcreem. He had little in the way of hair, so Bud chortled "What the HELL do you need that for?" EEEK!

Corey: My parents would quote him: "MOOOOOVE YOU COWS!"

Ann: I miss Bud's ... people don't shout in stores the way they used to!

Fred: Bud yelled at me. It was an honour.

Somerset at Preston

Somerset and Preston in the late '50s, looking east up Somerset from a spot just west of the intersection.

Shared by Don Frisby, this picture unleashed an avalanche of memories about living in the neighborhood.

Barry: My old stomping grounds. Preston and Somerset. I can still take you through that neighbourhood blindfolded. Our backyard on Booth Street had the 60-ton icicle running out of the natural stream from the rock formation. I have a picture of it taken in the mid-'50s.

Sheila: I know that icicle! And there are three small underground streams running straight into our basement on Anderson Street. Dang shale!

Barry: We used to have government folks and scientists coming into our yard to measure and take core samples. As a kid, we loved it. Used to slide down the old steel stairs that ran down Nanny Goat Hill.

Tom: I used to live at 129 Preston, and later at 85 Preston (in the '80s). Used to swim at the Plant Bath all the time. Best time of my life.

(SHARED BY DON FRISBY)

Barry: Remember the shacks at Plouffe Park in the winter? Change into skates and it cost a nickel to put your shoes and boots inside with the stove while you skated on the big outside rink and hockey was played on the inside?

Sandra: So much fun. I don't remember being charged to put our boots in the shack, though.

Barry: If you just left your boots in the main shack, you took a chance on them going missing, but for a nickel you could give them to Pop, the guy who ran the shacks and watered the ice. He would put them in the centre area where his office, so to speak, was located.

Sandra: I was raised on Bell near Somerset. Spent my life at Plouffe Park and Plant Bath. We skated all winter. We never came in except to eat and sleep. Such a wonderful place to live.

Chris: Azar's is an empty lot now but the other buildings look much the same.

Don: My dad used to take me to the pool hall just up the hill there when I was a kid ... some 40-plus years ago!

Barry: Capegreco's Cleaners was the first store on the north side of Somerset Street and the first store past the old White Rose gas station. Two stores to the left of this picture on Preston Street, there was Len's Barbershop. Len Martin and his grandfather Alf Langdon shared that spot for a few years.

Don: Thanks for mentioning Capegrecos Cleaners. Was it Louis Capegreco? Nice man.

Barry: Don, he and his family were the nicest folks in the area. We used to stand near the air vent when they were pressing clothes and laugh when the steam vented. Used to pretend the building was farting!

Philip: If you look real close you can see me in the back row of that eastbound streetcar, heading for the Somerset Theatre Saturday Matinee. Five-cent ride and 25 cents for the show.

Claudette: I can almost hear the "clang! clang!" of the street cars. They passed right in front of my grandmother's house on Albert Street. The CS Co-op is there now. When I slept over in the middle of the week, I would take one to get to school.

Lanny: My friend Mary Harris and I (her father, Frank, was a driver for the bus and streetcar routes) used to catch the streetcar at Bayswater and Somerset and take it all the way to Britannia and back home again. It was a bargain in those days. Kids' tickets were four for 25 cents — or six-and-a-quarter cents each way. You could have a lot of fun and create your own experience and memories for not much money in those days!

David: If I could only go back in time...

Ottawa Civic Hospital from the Air

This photo is looking southwest over the Ottawa Civic Hospital, not long after it opened in 1924, when the hospital was still called Fisher's Folly in honor of Mayor Harold Fisher (1917-1920) who had pushed for its construction on a site that seemed crazy far away, past even the outskirts of town.

Fisher was right though, and the city quickly expanded beyond the hospital's original location at Parkdale and Carling. As it grew, the Civic became ever more entwined with the lives of the thousands and thousands of people who were born there, worked there or recovered there.

That might help explain why this picture was so popular, another of our top three posts for 2013.

Gloria: It was called "Fisher's Folly" because it was so far from downtown, but now it's right in the middle of the city.

Manuja: Should be called "Fisher's Foresight" now!

John: They accounted for city expansion when they built this.

John: You mean we used to plan?

Nancy: Hard to believe the area was once so empty!

Kyrle: It was considered country back then, and my grandmother's farm was not too far away!

Lynda: Years ago, my friend Olive took me to what had been her home on Piccadilly. All around were sheep grazing in the middle of nowhere. Amazing.

Wayne: My uncle once mentioned that he would be bused in and out when he worked at the Civic as a teenager. They stayed there all week and were able to go home on weekends. He lived around Bronson and said the Civic was in the sticks. Now I believe him.

Lanny: When I moved to Ottawa as a six year-old, in 1953, Carling was a two-lane dirt road. We lived for a year on Archibald and I used to love visiting the Texaco station across Carling (where Westgate now stands) because they had two attractions in cages there — one was a bear; and the other were two monkeys. In 1955, we moved to Fern Avenue, a few blocks from the Civic. I remember that — at least to me — the city ended at Kirkwood to the west, and south at what is now multi-lane Baseline Road.

Mary: I used to work in the long building that runs along Parkdale, top right. Now it's the Civic-Parkdale Clinic, but it used to be the nurses' residence.

Bill: My mother graduated in nursing from the Civic in the '40s.

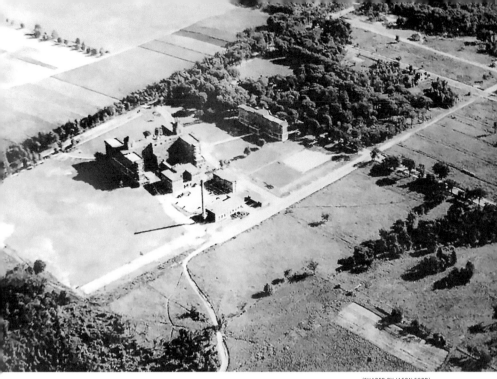

Judy: My Mother, Caroline (Bunny) Gormley, nee Smith, graduated from the Civic in 1924. She had fond memories of that time and nursed there for many years afterwards.

Scott: My Mom took her nurse's training at the Civic in the '50s.

Ian: My grandmother would have been a nursing student there around the same time.

Sherri: I lived in the residence in the mid-'70s. It was open to all girl students, not just nurses. Later, a floor was open to student doctors — both sexes.

John: My first appearance was at the Civic in 1954. Then came my children, 1972 to 1976! My mother, my daughter and I have all worked there.

Lori: I was born there in 1963. Both my kids were born there, too.

Ashlee: Ha! Same here!

Beverly: Husband works there. I was born there.

David: Never went near the place until my heart decided it needed to be bypassed. I quickly developed a fondness for the Ottawa Heart Institute and enjoyed its snack bar ... appropriately named "Tickers."

Andrea: But wait, they had all of this land and there is still barely any parking?

The Roundup

Started in 1888 and held in Lansdowne Park, the Central Canada Exhibition was an end-of-summer ritual that took place every year in late August.

Hundreds of thousands of people, millions maybe, attended the Ex over the years, until it closed in 2011.

Many people went for the food or the exhibits, and others for the rides. It was a memory of the rides that made me post this picture, taken at the Ex in 1970. I could not, however, quite remember the ride's name …

Lee: I believe it may have been called the "Roundup."

David: I'm sure it was called the Roundup. The ride where you lost all your change in your pockets.

Jacques: You stood along the edge of the "basket" and started spinning round and round, until the whole basket was 90-degrees to the pavement.

(ELIZABETH G. AMEY, COURTESY OF BRIAN STANTS)

Doug: It may have been called the "Vomit-Comet."

Alex: I always called it the Vomitron after an experience in 1993.

Doug: Puke Blaster!

David: Barf-a-tron comes to mind.

Susan: Ah, the Roundup ... the vomit would travel on this thing.

Gloria: It really took you for a ride. Made me sick.

Gail: This is the one where you stood up as it whirled around? If so — real sick!

Laura: On the Roundup you always ran the risk of having someone vomit on the other side of the circle and then it landing on you. Oh yes, good times!

Angie: The Roundup. I remember going on this ride at the Ex in Ottawa with my dad. He had false teeth. We got off the ride and he went to the garbage and got sick and had to pick his teeth out. He was a trooper. Despite his woozy stomach he rode it again!

Valerie: I went on that, and so did my step-dad, who immediately barfed in his own face — poor pops!

Lise: The Roundup was my favourite ride, although it was gross when people puked. You never knew who it would hit as we whizzed around!

Lynda: I went on this ride ONCE. Never went on a ride again.

Carolyn: There was also the "Tilt-a-Whirl," which I never went on, although my friends did. Some lost their cookies, and with the spinning you never knew who would get hit with it.

Jacques: The up and down and spinning around was a blast for me.

Victoria: I'm pretty sure it was called the Puke-a-Whirl.

Sean: Puke-a-Whirl!

Mike: My favourite Ex ride was the double Ferris wheel. Anyone remember that one?

Jean: Nice view from above!

Carol: Awesome.

Heather: The only ride that didn't make me sick! Loved it.

Robbin: At the end of August, just before we went back to school — the Ex was great way for us to wind down the summer with one last thrill. Too bad it's gone.

Richard: Blessed memories of walking the midway with friends and girlfriends — the lights, the music, the mix of sounds and smells, my God I miss those moments!

The Green Valley Restaurant

(SHARED BY DOMINIQUE PERRON)

The Green Valley Restaurant was one of the most popular posts of our first two months. Several months later, Dominique Perron shared this photo and people had even more to say about the Green Valley.

Started as a motor court in the 1930s, the Green Valley was located on the east side of Prince of Wales Drive, across from the Experimental Farm. The court with its cabins eventually disappeared, but the original diner grew into one of the city's most beloved dining establishments.

Under new ownership, the building burned down on New Year's Eve, 2002.

The restaurant may have died that night, but the memories certainly didn't!

Steve: "If you're really good until Sunday, we'll take you to the Green Valley." A very conservative ambience, even by the buttoned-down standards of the day, but the place to go for a special outing if you lived in the west end or City View, 1955 to 1970.

Jennifer: Anglo-Saxon food at its culinary finest. Really, really, Waspy. With turquoise banquettes and a basement gift shop, it was like walking into a Kraft Food commercial — but I would love to have a place like this to go to now.

Sheila: Every Sunday after church, it was either the Green Valley or the Red Door. I remember the gift shop so well. It must have been where my love of shopping began!

John: My parents' favourite restaurant. That and Imbro's for Italian food.

Joshua: Definitely an out-of-town-grandparents-will-take-you-as-a-treat kind of place. The minty ice cream with Mickey Mouse cookie ears was fab to a young boy in the 1970s. I still think of it when I drive past.

Michelle: If you asked me one thing I remember, it would be the Mickey Mouse ice cream.

Peter: I remember going for work lunches and sipping away on their signature "Gin Gimlets."

Lynn Robertson: First place I ever saw frog legs (taste like chicken) and turtle soup (tastes like chicken, too!).

Janice: My aunts took me there when I visited from Montreal and I remember the mushrooms on toast. Big yum!

Janet: And the lamb chops with mint sauce.

Kevin: Nut roll! Best Chicken Kiev in town.

John: Really good food, great roast duck. Not much atmosphere and a bit pricey, but did I mention REALLY GOOD FOOD!

Jo: I loved their pecan pie … yummy! It was great after a lovely family dinner.

Patricia: My fave was crème-de-menthe parfait!!

Skip: We ate there often, always dressed for dinner, and the wait-staff called my parents by name. It was nice.

Karen: My parents' 25th wedding anniversary was held there, as were other family celebrations. I still miss seeing it whenever we drive down Prince of Wales.

Lynda: Ate there at Christmas. So festive. It was a special place.

Marilyn: I remember trying to get in on a Mother's Day — no dice.

Jason: Sad to see it go!

Robert: It was an Ottawa institution!

The Traffic Noodle

September 24, 2013: 136 likes, 19 shares, 77 comments and 5,268 reached

The photo was shared by Phil Kinsman, who wrote: "View of Confederation Park in the winter of '71, with the sculpture "Traffic" in the foreground and the old DND temporary buildings behind, on the site of the current city hall. From a black-and-white photo I shot at the time."

Maggie: My dad worked at DND and he called this the "Continuous Turd!"

Stephen: Who can forget "The Turd."

Kirsten: I, too, always thought "Turd" when I was younger. As I got older I decided it looked like more like a colon (still loving that poo theme.)

Michael: We called it "Dino Poo!"

Karina: Laughing so hard over here! Thanks for posting this. I remember climbing on that thing, but we called it a sausage. I like "dinosaur turd" so much better! I needed this today!

Andrew: Alias the "Dinosaur Bowel" and "Big Turd."

John: What a piece of crap it was.

Reid: That's unkind to turds.

Wendy: I used to take the bus down Elgin and called this sculpture "The Movement."

Valerie: I think a lot of people called it "The Intestine."

Paula: We used to call it "The Worm."

Mika: "The Worm!" My favourite piece of public art ever! I once got stuck inside.

Sherry: Ugly is the only word I have for this so-called art.

Rob: My dad used to say it was like government. Started nowhere and ended nowhere.

Eric: I thought it was called "The Senate" — goes round and round and does nothing.

Rob: Funny, seeing this picture made me quite nostalgic. As a kid in the '70s, I thought this was beyond weird, and very out-of-place. But who knows? If it were still in Confederation Park, maybe we'd all like it by now. I wonder where it went?

Tristan: It was displayed from 1971-93, and is now in the National Gallery's storage.

Ann: Another piece of our history (good or bad) gone from sight.

Gloria: I always hated that thing.

Peter: I loved that sculpture!

Eve: I loved this thing when I went to Lisgar (High School.) We would go and sit on it and eat our lunches — a perfect example of successful public art where people could enjoy it not only aesthetically, but also engage with it physically. I'm so happy that it's still around.

Norma: I always liked it. And I was very impressed that the city I lived in (migrated to) was bold enough to install it. Made me proud.

JeanPaul: It is representative of '60s art in Western culture. It left few people indifferent, judging by the comments posted here!

Allan: Makes you realize how your perception of a work of art is so affected by the memories you associate with it. I remember having many a deep conversation within sight of this, so I have a fondness for it. I can certainly understand why others would have a different opinion.

Morris: What an iconic symbol of growing up in Ottawa in the '70s and '80s. Seeing this took me right back to my childhood!

Antoni: Love it or hate it, this stood out and inspired discussion.

Ottawa Skyline — 1859!

(LIBRARY AND ARCHIVES CANADA PA-120580)

Photography was just coming into common use in the late 1850s when this picture appears to have been taken by Montreal photographer William Notman.

It shows Parliament Hill before there was a Parliament on top, when the area was still known as Barracks Hill in memory of the British troops stationed there by Colonel By.

Below the Hill, in the foreground, square timber cribs are being re-assembled into rafts after passing down the timber slide between Amelia and Victoria Island – timber being the main business of Ottawa at this time.

On the left, below Nepean Point, are several buildings gathered around Sterling's Wharf, a small dockyard located at the bottom of the bluffs for more than a century. Above is the Convent of the Grey Nuns on Sussex, with Notre Dame Cathedral peeking out. To the right, atop Parliament Hill, are what appear to be the old barracks themselves.

All these buildings help date the picture. The spires were added to the cathedral in 1858 and construction of the Parliament Buildings started in 1859. So the photo seems to have been taken around that time.

People were still quite taken with the view, more than 150 years after it was captured. Good eye, Mr. Notman!

Molly: Wow! And with the Cathedral poking out from way behind! Awesome photo!

Gary: A great shot, really worth a 1,000 words.

Greg: Amazing to see the cathedral standing in the distance so many years before anything else.

Chantal: Didn't know the Cathedral was there before Parliament. Pretty cool!

Tracy: Cool. I'm putting this pic up in my Grade 8 history class tomorrow and I'll ask them where they think this is!

Sharon: What a precious record! I always find it incredible that photography existed this early.

Mark: The photographer would have been standing below the cliff where the Supreme Court now stands. This log-filled bay no longer exists. It was filled in and is now the hillside parking lot (and recreational path) below the Parliament Buildings.

Rob: I'm guessing pre-1859, since it doesn't look like construction on the Parliament Buildings has started.

Reta: Does anybody know if the building to the left of the Cathedral is the old hospital? I found that it burned in 1928, but I could not find when it was built.

Max: That is the convent of the Grey Nuns.

Pat: The old General Hospital was originally called Water St. Hospital. I was born there and then had my tonsils out there when I was six years old!

Richard: I miss seeing the logs floating down the river.

Robert: Even in my youth, in the late '60s and '70s, I remember the logs on the Ottawa River. I've thought for a long time that some of the old Eddy land in Hull should be used for a logging museum that tells the in-depth story of Ottawa's logging history.

Scott: Years ago, when Jean Pigott was still head of NCC, it was one of her pet dreams to have the E.B. Eddy buildings restored and made into a museum. Unfortunately, I doubt that will happen in this day and age, but if this were still the '60s and '70s, oh, par chance to dream.

Hobbyland

Sometimes there is such a thing as synchronicity. Which is what happened on November 6, 2013, when the stars aligned for this post.

First came a post of a book for Matchbox dinky toys, stamped with the name of the Hobbyland store that was once located at the corner of Slater and O'Connor Streets.

Then came a newspaper advert for Hobbyland (not to be confused with Hobby House out Montreal Road).

Third, came an actual picture of Hobbyland taken by Norm Macleod and shared by Laurel Dewan, who wanted to know if anyone remembered it.

Andy: Best hobby store in Ottawa.

Carla: My dad would take me every Saturday afternoon. Best place ever.

Nata: I remember the Meccano sets and the trains.

Richard: I bought HO train stuff there, when I was a kid.

Karin: My father used to shop here, and occasionally he would bring one or two of us kids along. He had a model railroad hobby. They had an incredible assortment of HO and N scale.

Gilles: We bought our balsa wood there. It was flying model airplanes HQ. Control lines and R/C, Cox motors, etc. They had it all!

Jennifer: I bought my first model airplane here!

Skip: I spent many happy hours in this place, when the car model craze was hitting its stride.

Dave: I used to go almost every Saturday to look at or buy AMT model cars. I won a couple of contests with my models around 1960.

Michael: Fifty years ago, I purchased Dinky toys there, subsequently destroyed by sand piles and firecrackers. I am collecting the same toys again, mint-in-box, and find myself paying several hundred dollars apiece. The original price at Hobbyland was 85 cents!

Patrice: I loved that store, I can still feel the atmosphere it had when you stood in the narrow aisles full of model kits, games, R/C planes on the wall behind the counter, trains, Dungeons and Dragons pamphlets before they were hardcover. What a strong memory I have of it.

Lanny: I remember the store well because I was a young single parent in the late 60s (divorced after just a couple of years, which was not the

thing to do in those days). I had to leave my young son with a babysitter, as they were called then. Hobbyland was only a block from my office at Metcalfe and Slater and every Friday, for three or four years, I would go in and buy a toy to bring home for my son to enjoy on the weekend. Most were very inexpensive. Small kids don't need a lot. He and I would enjoy playing with the newest toy, until he was old enough for models. Then he became an avid customer himself, spending his allowance and birthday money at the store!

Darrell: They moved to 93 O'Connor after the Saturday, October 25, 1958 gas explosion that leveled the Jackson Building.

Robert: I remember when the original store was leveled by the explosion in the Jackson Building. All of us neighbourhood kids went rummaging through the Hobbyland ruins, making out like bandits, finding scores of toys and models in good condition, if you were willing to dig for them. Those of us who attended Kent Street Public School had some free time on our hands after the explosion, because all the windows in our school were blown out.

Frank: Sounds like it was a Kent Street Public inside job to me.

Robert: Ya do what ya gotta do, Frankie!

Ponderosa Steak House

— Journal-CP

Ponderosa restaurant on Bank Street: Homeowners unhappy

(OTTAWA CITIZEN)

Restaurant chains come and go and Ponderosa Steak House was one of them. This picture was posted by Glen Gower; along with a link to a story about Ponderosa at Ottawastart.com.

The story had to do with a neighborhood dispute about cooking odors, but members of Lost Ottawa had their own set of memories

Garey: "Square meal, square deal — Ponderosa!"

Judy: Ponderosa is one of the first places I can remember that started the salad bar thing.

Janet: Imagine a steak dinner for $1.29! We would spend $5 for two of us and go home stuffed!

Debbie: I used to go to the St. Laurent location as a kid. It really bugged me when we went right after I got my braces tightened. Steaks too hard to chew for sore teeth!

Carolyn: Ponderosa was my first job. I loved working there. I was the bun girl.

Karin: My first job at 15 was at the Ponderosa on Montreal Road. Ridiculous uniforms.

Joseph: My first job was at the St. Laurent location. I was a bus boy and worked the buns-and-drink station. It was the first time I came across an all-you-can-eat salad bar. And then I found out the cobbler was just unsold pieces of pie, crushed up with whip cream on top.

Lee: I worked at a Ponderosa in '74, making $1.45 an hour. Cut off the end of my index finger in the lettuce slicer. Lifetime reminder!

Joseph: Oh yeah, memories coming back. The lettuce slicer was awesome ... until I watched the heads of lettuce go right out of the box off the truck and into the slicer BUGS AND ALL.

Chris: I was the grill cook at the St. Laurent location in 1979-80. That was the one that got robbed. I had a big pistol stuck in my face, had to lie on the ground with eyes shut and hands behind my head. I also remember huge tubs of lettuce we had to pour pounds of MSG into in order to preserve it, and slicing open my finger and bleeding all over the prime rib. People kept eating it ...

Brien: I worked at the Merivale and Baseline location in 1982-83. Nothing like working over a hot greasy grill in a polyester "jeans" shirt and hat! Started at $2.65 hour, as I recall. I still draw on my extensive training to make the diamond pattern with steaks on the barbecue.

Lynda: The steaks had a funny taste. I think they used to cook them in some kind of synthetic butter. I can taste it now. Yuck.

Theresa: Anyone remember the rumour that they used kangaroo meat and that's why it was so cheap?

Chris: I recall when I worked there being told it was New Zealand dairy cattle, packed in meat tenderizer for the journey.

Glenn: Anyone else call it Ponde-gross-a?

Amos: I remember going there as a kid for my birthday dinner. Loved it, miss it ... in some weird way.

Mike: Some childhood memories are meant to remain just memories. We went to a Ponderosa in Florida in January of 2013 ... it was awful.

Ski-joring Anyone?

This was the Picture of the Month for November 2013. It shows two people in bathing suits "skijoring" during an Ottawa Winter, circa 1930.

I had to look that one up, discovering that "skijoring" is the Anglicized word for a Norwegian "sport" in which you were towed on skis behind dogs, horses, cars, or even motorcycles. Who knew?

In my day, we skipped the skis and towropes for what we called "bunking." With enough snow on the road, or enough ice underneath, we grabbed the bumper of a car passing by and got towed along in our boots, whether the drivers wanted to tow us or not.

Even more astonishing, we survived!

Siri: I've done this many times with horses and it's great fun.

Nancy: We used toboggans. No helmets. Just good old fun!

Jon: We were raised near Chelsea. My father took us skijoring quite often behind our '53 Ford along the Scott Road, north of Old Chelsea.

(CANADA SCIENCE AND TECHNOLOGY MUSEUM CN CP-6642)

Stephen: We survived bunking … but there was always that story your mom told you about the kid who lost a finger bunking an OTC bus.

Thomas: In Winnipeg we called it "bumper shining."

Claude: On the other side of the river we called it "skiboots."

Frieda: I remember bunking. In my neighborhood, only the boys did that. My mother would have killed my brothers if she caught them at it.

Jan: I've told people outside of Ottawa about me bunking around the Glebe in the early '60s and they are usually amazed anyone would indulge in that kind of risky behaviour. It seemed like fun at the time. Nothing I ever suggested to my own kids …

Dennis: I remember bunking. Crazy and extremely dangerous.

Richard: Guilty as charged! Behind a snowmobile with my best friend, Stephane.

Marilyn: In my days, the boys were brave enough to even bunk the backs of streetcars.

Don: Quite often behind the Morrison Lamothe truck.

Jennifer: I remember bunking OTC buses over the Bank Street Bridge to get to school faster!

Heather: I used to watch the boys bunk on Elgin street all the way over the Pretoria Bridge to Ottawa East. I tried it once for a few feet, fell off and was nearly run over by a bus. It is amazing we survived such lunacy!

Garry: Bunking on Elgin Street was the best.

Glenn: Back in the '70s, OTC had these buses that ran through Crystal Beach, Lakeview and Bells Corners, maybe a few other places, every half hour. You called in, it showed up at your house, and you took it directly to Bayshore Shopping Center. We called it "Dial-a-Bunk," but I admit the driver caught on fairly quickly. We would call the bus to a house near where the driver liked to enter the neighborhood, jump on and tour the neighborhood for a while. We got pretty good at it. We could ride all the way to Bayshore if no one knew we were there. My mom lost her patience with it all when I kept wearing holes in my boots and shoes. Bare pavement patches wore your boots out fast, because falling at speed was not an option. Amazing that we are still here to talk about it!

Scott: I almost wish I hadn't been such a sane kid.

Glenn: We even had one driver, if he knew we were there, and no one else was on the bus, that would give us a "Hell Ride," sliding on corners trying to knock us off into the snowbanks. It was a huge amount of fun.

Allan: Bunking? Only bad kids did that.

Edmund: Guess I was a bad kid.

Royal Burger

The Royal Burger was Ottawa's very own burger chain, started by Reg Bruce and partner Lou MacDonald (of Bruce MacDonald Motor Hotel fame).

The first one opened on Richmond Road in 1960. Four more opened over the next several years, including this one on Montreal Road in 1961.

In those days, teenage life was all about cars, which meant drive-ins were all the rage and Royal Burger was on the cutting edge.

By '73 they were out of business, but people sure remember them — and the secret sauce!

Fergus: They had the best burgers in the world! Nothing close to it anywhere.

Barry: It wasn't so much the burgers but the sauce that was the trick.

Diane: I remember their special sauce. It made for the best hamburger, for me, to this day. Anyone have the recipe?

Dave: Mustard and ketchup mixed half and half.

Ann: Equal parts finely chopped onion and dill pickle, ketchup and mustard. Mix together.

James: I worked at the Richmond Road location as a teen and remember making the "Special Sauce" in five-gallon pails. We would pour all the ingredients in the pail, then stir it with one arm fully immersed in the product.

Sherry: My husband and I lived right across the street from this one when we got married in the fall of '67, although we had been going to the Royal Burger years before that. The two-patty burger was 60 cents and the one-patty burgerette was 25 cents. Best onion rings EVER.

Barb: We loved the Royal Burger on Richmond Road. My husband and I (boyfriend at the time) went there every Friday night.

Debby: We used to go the Royal Burger on Richmond Road all the time when I was a kid. I loved their hot dogs.

Wayne: I worked at the one on Richmond Road — for two nights. All I did was make onion rings! But the food was good!

Michael: The Royal Burger was a family favorite for sure. They invented the drive-thru concept in Ottawa. We'd eat in the car and when the trains went by along the river blowing their horn, my brother would dive under the seat (he was terrified of trains).

Barry: I worked for a year at the one on Carling at Woodroffe. Friday and Saturday nights were a madhouse, as folks going to the Britannia Drive-In would make a food run before the second feature. I remember once making 25 Royales for a single order.

Dave: We hung out at the one on Bank Street with my '53 Chevy convertible, after going to the Britannia Drive-In.

Wendy: My husband (boyfriend then) and I used to hang out at Bank Street with friends from Brookfield and Ridgemont (high schools.) The guys would show off their cars and talk about whose was fastest.

Lynn: My husband proposed to me in the line-up! We celebrated our 50th anniversary this year.

Pierre: Four years after we were married in '64, we rented an apartment in Hull on the street where the Royal Burger was built (from prefab components in less than a week). Thereafter, every evening until the wee hours, we were treated to "Yeah!" and "with the works" and wonderful phrases like that, never to be forgotten. Wonderful memories!

Bus Transfer

December 16, 2013: 265 likes, 47 shares and 50 comments

Remember when bus transfers looked like this? The bus driver would put a stack of them upside down in a big clip, angling them so the sharp edge would rip the paper at just the right "expiry" time.

When you changed buses you had to decide whether to give it to the driver or keep it, and there was the omnipresent chance of your time running out.

This transfer from the mid-'80s was shared by Marie Aline Oliver.

Mike: Wow. Haven't seen these in forever. Vintage!

Marie: A reminder of my hundreds of hours riding the 95.

Alex: They would always be fiddling with the transfer time edger just when you needed the bus to leave ASAP.

Tania: And you could only use them for one direction, no double-backs!

Jean: Those were the days before the bus passes.

Chad: I think I still have a monthly student pass somewhere. I loved those. It made a student feel important because of the two parts in a slipcover. Kinda like flashing a badge.

Judith: I have a whack of bus passes from the '80s. When they were CHEAP!

Nadine: I remember the transfers from a trip I took on an 86, and then tried to switch to the 85. Because the hole was between the 5 and the 6 the driver wouldn't let me on. I despised those POP transfers — but enjoyed only paying $1.85!

Robert: I asked for a transfer and the driver didn't respond. I thought he didn't hear me so I asked again. He swore at me and threatened to kick me off his "goddam bus!"

Fiona: I still have one somewhere.

Frank: As a driver, I still have a set.

Chantal: My dad used to bring them home from work before a shift. I had to help him punch them all!

Dave: My dad, who was an OC Transpo driver, used to give me transfers and a puncher to get on the buses for free in '96.

Grahame: I've got a whole stack of these in my mom's basement. I used to keep them for some reason.

Jennifer: I still have a couple hidden in a book. I remember trying to alter them so that I could use it on the return trip!

Joseph: We used to keep all our transfers because, if you flashed the right colour and time rip on the right day, the driver never questioned it.

Ava: I remember! They used different colours daily.

Linda: Every day a different colour, and at the end of the day, you would always get an extra long one so you could transfer — but you better not miss your connection!

Jill: I remember a girl who saved them all. Her sister would call her when she got to work and tell her what colour they were using that day. She would pull out a transfer from her colour-coded pile for the right time, right bus and direction. It was hysterical to watch her work her system. She sure saved on bus fare though.

Tina: Ah, the smell of a fresh transfer! Mmmmm.

Adam: You know, this doesn't seem that long ago. I remember that if you licked the empty green strip in the time area there were invisible watermarks that would reveal themselves.

Bruce: I think that was called acid.

Adam: We were teenagers, and teenagers do ridiculous things! I believe a friend showed me what happened if you licked them. The messages were along the general theme of "Ride The Bus!" so of course we assumed they were meant as subliminal messages!

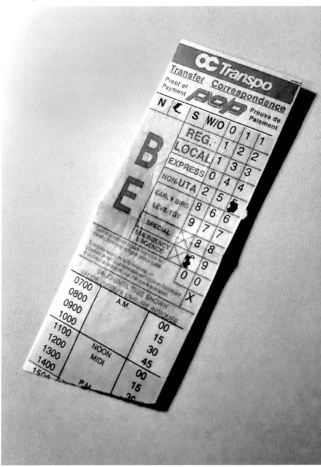

(SHARD BY MARIE ALINE OLIVER)

The Green Valley Again

March 24, 2013: 349 likes, 84 shares and 220 comments

Stewart's Green Valley Restaurant was located on what was then known as the Prescott Highway (now Prince of Wales.) It was about one-third of the way between Baseline Road and the roundabout by the Experimental Farm.

From the '50s on, the Green Valley was one of the few classy joints in town, with white tablecloths and proper cutlery, a place where everyone dressed up, and kids minded their manners.

Everyone who went there agrees it was THE place for special occasions: birthdays, anniversaries, wedding receptions, visits from out of town friends and relatives, tea with grandma — and let's not forget the Mickey Mouse ice cream! So it was with a heavy heart that people learned it had burned to the ground on New Year's Eve, 2002.

Our post of the Green Valley was the first one where we could watch it grow in "real time," seeing the number of likes and comments increase with every refresh of the browser. The post was so popular we decided to add a second picture of the inside of the restaurant.

Together, the two pictures garnered 349 Likes, 84 shares and 220 comments. Since there were only 250 members of Lost Ottawa at the time, we were amazed to see the number of people who viewed the picture reach 16,000. It was the first time we really said to ourselves, "maybe we're onto something here."

Shawn: There was a time when the Chateau Laurier and the Green Valley were the only white tablecloth joints in town, assuming you weren't a member of the House of Commons, the Rideau Club, or the Cercle.

Judy: I went there so many times as a child, and then as an adult. We all dressed in our Sunday finest.

Janet: That was the spot in town where children learned their adult table manners.

Margaret: We would have "Mother's Day" lunch there when I was very young. Best behaviour was totally expected. Sad to hear that it is no longer.

Carolyn: My mother-in-law took us, and our children, when they were one and four -years old. All dressed up and well behaved — thank goodness.

Valerie: When I was little, it was THE place to go for Sunday dinner with my parents and grandparents, all dressed up fancy in my patent leather shoes and velvet dress.

Theresa: Our celebratory end-of-the-school-year dinner was always here.

Mike: I remember New Year's Eve — they had a band.

Karin: Many couples had their wedding receptions there, including my husband's Italian aunt and uncle. "Little Italy" was very close.

Janice: Had my wedding reception there in the '70s.

Judy: My wedding rehearsal dinner was held there in 1970.

Sandy: I had my first fancy date there. I believe we had to take a bus because my date didn't have a car. I wasn't very nice to him ... shame on me!

Sheila: My parents went there each year on their anniversary, just the two of them. They are coming up on 65 years married this summer. Broke their hearts when it burned down.

Terry: Sunday was for high tea!

Sheri: Yes! Special place for "tea" with nanny when she came to town!

Michael: Bought my first car on Bank Street in 1957 — a VW Bug and I only knew one way to drive out of Ottawa. This went past the Green Valley and since I had already spent a huge amount of money that I didn't have ($1,300) I thought I would top it off by going in and having a great dinner that cost me an arm and a leg ($3.00?).

Ivor: Prime rib of beef was AMAZING here.

Tom: Ah yes, those Sunday bunches after the 11:30 mass at Saint Augustine's, when you couldn't eat for three hours before mass. My stomach growling by communion time, and that little white host didn't do the trick. But the Green Valley roast-beef? NOW THAT WAS MEAT! Melt in your mouth. Mmmm!

Linda: My husband grew up in the neighborhood and his dad supplied the Green Valley with fresh berries from his garden. My first taste of Chateaubriand was there. Boy did I think I was something!

Lee: I remember eating there a couple of times as a kid, when it was a huge treat to go out for dinner. First place I had frog legs and grasshopper pie. Loved them both.

Maggie: This was where I ate vichyssoise for the very first time and was so surprised that it was COLD!

Jill: I went there many times over the years. As a child and as an adult, and I always ordered the same thing. It was so delicious, noon or night. Mushrooms on toast, with cheese sauce and a side salad. YUM!

Martha: The Green Valley was the first restaurant we went to when we moved to Ottawa from Nova Scotia. My mom loved the gift shop and the creamed mushrooms on toast. I loved the Shirley Temples.

Greg: My grandmother would take us there as a treat on a regular basis. They had the best liver and onions in town! After dinner we would browse the fabulous gift shop.

John: Liver and onions! Delivered by a waitress who always called you "dear."

Judy: The waitresses, from my memory, all had grey-blue hair and were senior. It was very much the place to take the granny.

Lois: Its nickname was "Blue Hair Haven" because of all the older people who dined there!

Sue: My cousins Cindy and Sandy would go with my brother Rob and me, courtesy of grandmother, and we had the Mickey Mouse special. Grandmother always ordered, not the famous roast beef but ... LIVER! She'd say: "I'll have the liver and an Old-Fashioned!" Mum would have a Manhattan and something else. All of my grandmother's daughters would say, "Mum, why the liver? Look at the other nice dishes on the menu!" But she'd just nod and smile ...

2014

Toboggan Slide at the Chateau Laurier

The date was 1922. Ottawa had been through the Great War and the hard economic times that followed. What better time to revive the Winter Carnival? And what could be better for a Winter Carnival than a giant toboggan run beside the Chateau Laurier?

Starting at street level, riders accelerated down the hill beside the locks and rocketed out into the middle of the Ottawa River at 60 miles-per-hour until they reached the Alexandra Bridge. "Slide a mile for a dime" went the slogan.

(LIBRARY AND ARCHIVES CANADA PA-012648)

Governor General Lord Byng sent the first toboggan down the run. On the toboggan were Mayor Frank Plant and businessman A.J. Major, and two other gentlemen (The GG did not partake.)

Readers loved the idea of this ride and were of two opinions. One was how much fun it would be. The other was, bring back the slide!

Marilyn: My mom and dad used to enjoy this.

Andrea: Looks like you used to be able to have fun in Ottawa! Wish they still did this.

Sharon: It would bring some life and a healthy pastime to the downtown.

Pat: The NCC should bring that toboggan run back!

Ron: Or Parks Canada.

Patrick: I think the NCC did try to get the slide going again in the mid-'90s with the help of sponsorship from the RBC, but costs made it prohibitive.

Wendy: What an attraction it would be!

Jason: And sooooo much fun!

Toon: A good way to keep and entertain tourists in the city core, something our city needs! And a better use of that space than the shuttered. photography museum that's there now.

Claude: I would love to go down on a skeleton sled.

Maryanne: Looks scary, but love the Union Jack!

Sylvie: Imagine how great it would be if it still existed!

Tania: Fastest way to get to Hull?

Lucie: I would say so!

Rob: I wish they could bring this back but, with climate change, I don't think the river would be able to hold that weight coming on to it anymore. It's not like the old days when we had real winters!

Susan: It would never happen now.

Phyllis: Today there would be too many rules. You'd need helmets, protective gear, special sliders, sign a waiver, etc. Then if anyone got hurt, everyone would be condemning whoever came up with this idea.

Carya: I would love to see something like this again. Too bad most parents have to bubble wrap their children these days!

Christine: So many fun things taken away. I feel like we live in a protective bubble, because the government is afraid that people will get hurt.

Carrie: You are sooooo right.

Steve: Exactly! Nobody is allowed to have fun anymore!

(LIBRARY AND ARCHIVES CANADA PA-012630)

Britannia Drive-In

March 21, 2014: 565 likes, 194 shares, 73 comments and 4,896 reached

One of the most popular posts on Lost Ottawa in 2014 was a shot of the big screen of the Britannia Drive-in, located on the south side of Carling, near Bayshore Drive.

When it first opened in 1948, the Britannia was in the boonies, surrounded by farmland, but as the city grew the drive-in wove its way into the fabric of Ottawa life.

For young and old, going there was an experience never to be forgotten. It was, however, an experience that eventually came to an end, when the big outdoor screen was replaced with a mega-plex in 1997.

Susan: Boy, do I miss the Britannia Drive-in! We used to live on the other side of the back fence, where (with the owner's permission) all the neighbours had their own "sound box" hooked up to the house. In good weather or bad, it was great to have friends over, make popcorn and watch the movie ... FOR FREE! This was about 1965.

(GeoOttawa)

Gilles: I remember going to Britannia as a kid. Nothing like watching a movie in the back of the station wagon in my pjs.

Sandra: Loved going there ... in my jammies.

Catherine: My parents took us to movies there in the station wagon. We popped our own popcorn and brought our own drinks.

Barb: Always loved the drive-in theaters, which were a very inexpensive way to spend an evening with the family. You could bring your own treats and drinks. On long weekends they had the dusk-to-dawn movies. Great fun!

Chris: Great times as kids. Dad would take us there in his Hemi GTX. We would throw a Frisbee or football while the beverages mellowed in the cooler before the show.

Linda: Those were the days — the speaker hanging beside the car, stretching out on the hood of the car with pillows, a comfy blanket, the smell of hot dogs and popcorn from the concession stand, and then the rush we got, trying to be the first car out.

Tom: A time in history for many of us ... like that one long weekend, at an all-nighter, getting locked out of the car with lights flashing and horns honking. Oh, did I mention we were streaking ...

Mike: Used to sit on the fence with friends and watch the movies.

Sandra: Used to crawl under the fence with a blanket and watch the movies.

Jen: I hid in the trunk.

Donna: Grew up there! We would go in a gang and socialize from car to car. Loved it! I remember going to the all-nighters and then for breakfast in the morning. Fell in love with James Darren and watched Gidget and Beach Blanket Bingo!

Chrissy: I remember watching E.T. on the hood of the car there.

Robert: My mom and dad took me to see Jaws there when I was about 10, traumatizing me for the rest of my life.

Donna: Whoa, brings me back. Ten in a van (with carpet on the ceiling) watching Rocky Horror and Cheech and Chong at the midnight show!

Andy: I can't remember the movies I saw there. I was too busy doing something else.

Bram: Great place to take the kids ... and tell them where they came from.

Kim: Unfortunately, I never made out there. The guys wanted to watch the movie! What it this world coming to!?

Longest Bar in the Gatineau

Ottawa has a long history of drinking on the Quebec side of the river, whether it was in Hull, out the Aylmer Road, or up in the Gatineau Hills.

One favorite drinking hole was the Kazubazua Hotel, about an hour's drive north of the city on Quebec route 105. It featured "The Longest Bar in the Gatineau."

Shown here about 1960, "the Kaz" was destroyed by fire in July of 2002.

Cindy: Owned by my cousin, once or twice removed. Last name Payette.

Lee: This was a regular stop on the weekend, going up to fish in the Maniwaki area.

Brian: At one time they had a fish tank, where husbands could buy fresh fish to take home and show their wives that they had, indeed, been fishing.

Gerry: I had a quart there ... or ten. Sorely miss the old place.

Yves: We used to close the Carousel at Sinclair Lake at midnight, go for a beer at the Brennan's Hill Hotel, then another one at Ray's in Low, then hit the Longest Bar, and return to Brennan's Hill to rally the gang for a party at Lion's Lake (Scout Camp Stanislas) to finish the night.

Stephen: Wakefield Inn, Brennan's Hill, Venosta, Kaz, Riverside, Danford. Our kids will never know that much fun!

Gilles: Drinking and driving was in then. Thank God, not anymore.

Robert: My dad and his brothers used to go there. I was too young, and stayed outside feeding the black bear in the cage.

Conrad: Played there with my band.

Cath: OMG. Spent my teenage years there. So much fun. Ernie and the Overnight Ramblers were there for years and years.

Lance: Wow. I'm sure I played there.

Robert: Our band was going to play there, but it burned down two weeks before our booking.

Karen: Looks a lot brighter than I remember.

Anneke: And what ubiquitous items in this photo are no longer ubiquitous?

Leona: I'd say ashtrays are no longer ubiquitous. Not even there ... thankfully!

Anneke: Funny how easy it is to forget the joys of sitting around in clouds of cigarette-smoke. Not!

Leona: This must be a noontime (or breakfast) shot, before the place was taken over with cigarette smoke! The chairs remind me of the Carleton Tavern, a place I spent way too much time in — on the ladies and escorts side, of course. Whenever I go there now, it still feels wrong to sit on the "men's" side.

Sheelagh: The good old days! Just an empty lot now.

Marc: WAS on my bucket list.

Hopscotch on Bruyère Street

Hopscotch was the main game where I went to grade school and I still remember obsessing about the chain we would use to make our throws into the right squares (often a chain stolen from one of those old pull-chain lamps or light sockets at home).

So I couldn't resist this picture of an Ottawa youngster playing hopscotch on Bruyére Street, near King Edward, circa 1960. It really got people thinking about the games they played as kids.

Sheryl: I played hopscotch endlessly with friends. Getting the right chain was crucial!

Lorraine: We played hopscotch with rocks, but if you were lucky you found a ball chain to use instead. Didn't bounce as much.

Neil: I remember kids did this in the Glebe ... and someone called the city to clean it up.

Tasha: Glashan Public had hopscotch games painted in the girls' side of the yard in the late '60s. My favourite was one that looked like a snail. We had the one that was "straight up," with both single and double blocks, so you sometimes hopped on one foot, sometimes two. That was the standard version?

Sandra: I played that one all the time, back in the '50s. First three blocks were singles, four and five were side by side, six was single, seven and eight were doubles, with nine at the top. Sometimes we went to twelve, and it was just one box with an "X" in it.

Isabel: When I was a kid in the '50s we played hopscotch, red rover, marbles, skipping rope, mother may I, and on and on. We were always outside.

Eileen: I grew up playing hopscotch in the '50s. It was the "in" game along with red rover, elastic skipping, double Dutch and Chinese skipping, and marbles (we called them allies.) Oh yes, jacks!

Michelle: This one in the picture is the version I remember from the '60s. I also remember elastic, red rover, tether ball, swings, and monkey bars. All the things that could seriously hurt you. We went to the nurse's office for a bandage and moved on.

Barb: When I started school in '61 we played hopscotch, red rover, skipping, baseball, dodge ball, and Simon says.

Anneke: We played hopscotch, and donkey (a ball game with those red, white and blue rubber balls thrown against the school wall) as well as

baseball and soccer in the schoolyard. We skipped ... but I could never double Dutch.

Tasha: I absolutely loved elastic — think it was my favourite schoolyard game.

Caroline: A packet of those little coloured elastics meant hours of fun!

Lynne: I bet kids today don't even know what elastic is.

Cathy: Thanks for reminding me of the elastic game! We would sing this nonsense rhyme: "Yoki and the Kaiser, Yoki addy ay, Tamba, so-ba, Sa-du, say-day. Yoki in the Kaiser, Yoki allee-ay, Kick him in the so-po, Sa-du, sa-day!" Or something like it ...

Louise: OMG. I forgot about that!

Barry: The big game on the boys' side was "card closest to wall." Tips, corners, and fully covered. I remember bringing 200-to-300 cards from baseball to hockey to sports of all kinds. We used to get 10 cards in a pack, and pink bubblegum that was so hard you could cut yourself — but the smell was fantastic!

Laurel: Do kids even play hopscotch anymore?

Debi: I run a daycare and we still play hopscotch ... in the 21st Century!

1964 Dodge

Lost Ottawa contributor Brian Woodard and his father were having a big day on May 26, 2014.

That was the 50th anniversary of the day this beautiful '64 Dodge hardtop was purchased from Steinberg Motor Sales in Williamsburg, just south of Ottawa.

For it's Golden Anniversary the car was heading back to the same dealership to be professionally photographed and written up for an article in a car magazine.

Beverley: We had a blue '64 Dodge, four doors though. Push button transmission. That was neat!

Dianne: Very cool. We had three '60s Dodges back in college days, one with a push button. Loved them all.

Eric: I am thinking the 1958 Ford Edsel started the pushbutton (Teletouch) transmission craze ...

Dave: My grandfather's '56 Dodge was push button. The first year Chrysler did that.

Brian: I believe the push button transmission was a Chrysler innovation that began in '55, when Virgil Exner came up with the "forward look" designs.

Beverley: The push button transmissions weren't very popular, I guess. Never saw another one after we got rid of the Dodge.

Brian: Push buttons were pretty much a Chrysler feature only – until push button transmissions were outlawed in 1965. Other manufacturers tended to use column-mounted shifters like the ones used today.

Cheryl: An old friend of my father owned one just like this. He was one of the original Nepean Township police force members.

Skip: Time capsule!

Garry: I recognized this beauty as soon as I saw it. First time was back in '77.

Brian: It would have belonged to Marcel Renaud back then. He owned it from October '66 up to August '86.

Garry: Marc used to bring this car into work to wash on Sunday at old Number 1 Station. I worked with your grandfather there as well, Brian.

Brian: He would bring it in to wash it, and all the firefighters would put breadcrumbs on the windshield so birds would come and poop on the glass!

Audie: I notice there's no Steinberg Motor Sales in Williamsburg anymore.

Brian: Steinberg went out of business in '81. However, the original business partners, Paul Steinberg and Mac Strader, had already split up in '69. Paul kept Steinberg and Mac went on to start Strader Motors in Morrisburg, which is still in business today.

Annette: My father-in-law bought a Monaco 500 at Steinberg Motor Sales in '69. He factory-ordered the car with a stick shift but it came with an armrest instead! He wasn't happy about it, so they offered to exchange the car for a '68 Dodge Super Bee that came with a stick. In the end he decided to take the Monaco. Too bad!

(SHARED BY BRIAN WOODARD)

Civic Pharmacy Sign

(LOST OTTAWA)

The Civic Pharmacy, on the corner of Carling and Holland, was once a haven for travelers seeking shelter from the elements as they waited for their Ottawa Transportation Commission bus to arrive ... or not.

Anneke D. who shared the original picture, vividly recalled the experience:

"When I was in Grade 5 (1966/67) at Elmwood, I usually had to take the bus home, and anyone who remembers the buses in the late '60s knows what a horrific experience that was.

At Holland and Carling, the slush in the turn-around was usually so deep you had to stand in it up to your ankles, freezing your feet off the whole time you were there.

The one saving grace was the Civic Pharmacy, across the street. When my feet were in danger of falling off from the cold, I would go in and peruse the magazine rack in front of the big window that overlooked Holland, glancing out to check for my bus.

I attended Elmwood for a year but we moved to New Edinburgh in February '67, so the bus ordeal only lasted a few months. It seemed a lifetime to me.

A note about the Civic sign: Those big Popsicle letters used to rotate. I always feel sad when I pass the building because I love that sign and know that one day it will be gone."

Reid: I have always been fascinated with that sign for some reason. I too remember the days when the letters turned.

Gordon: I remember them rotating. Wish they still did today.

Chris: I love this sign. It was made by Azar Signs, when the company was located at the corner of Preston and Somerset. The transom has a gold leaf address, which is still there. Azar did a lot of backlit and neon from the early-'50s to the mid-'80s.

Gord: Stood under that sign for what seemed like forever waiting for the 2 or 2a Laurier to arrive.

John: I waited there many, many, times for the 71 to go home, or the 5 or 6 to go downtown to work.

Peter: I remember when the Civic Pharmacy and the adjoining Civic Restaurant was a cluttered vacant lot at Holland and Carling Avenues. I used to live at 1127 Carling Avenue, just west of there, and remember the beige brick pharmacy very well (sigh).

Anne: We used to feel so grown-up when we ate at the Civic Restaurant.

Lise: That used to be my transfer point on the bus when I was traveling downtown from Parkwood Hills. The restaurant made the best fries!

Nancy: This was an iconic spot when I lived on Holland Avenue, with the restaurant in the same building ... and the best French fries!

Beryl: I remember freezing in the bus shelter at that very corner. The over-crowded buses kept passing as I wept from pain. Although I was wearing winter boots, my toes were freezing. One reason why I had to move away from Ottawa was the humidity, but the other was the unrelenting bone-chilling temperature.

Donna: I took those buses often. By the time I got on the third one, I was feeling carsick and had to get off before my stop and walk.

Ginette: Ah, yes. Back in the days when doctors would tell you not to smoke, then cross over to the Civic Pharmacy to buy themselves a pack of cigarettes.

Two Highways to Nowhere

When the Macdonald-Cartier Bridge connecting Ottawa to Hull opened in 1965, it was supposed to connect directly to the Queensway via a new King Edward expressway, and indirectly to the Queensway via the Vanier Parkway (following the route of the old railway bridge across the Rideau River that you can see in the picture).

Neither of these things happened, resulting in one of the city's worst traffic nightmares, as trucks traveling up King Edward are forced to make a hard right turn onto Rideau, and then a hard left to zigzag around the Rideau Centre to get onto Nicholas and (eventually) onto the highway.

It doesn't seem to have occurred to planners that people would oppose the carving up of their neighborhoods for highways, but that's what happened. It's still a touchy subject!

Simon: Ah, good old Ontario. Let's have a massive freeway connection to ... nothing.

Trevor: Sadly, common sense and proper planning in this city are not common themes.

Dan: New Edinburghers lobbied long and hard to save the park behind Crichton Street and have the highway project axed. That's why the Vanier Parkway is a four-lane highway till you get to Beechwood, where it suddenly stops. Not sure why they can't use St. Patrick, which seems like a natural route that hooks up with King Edward. Anyone?

Benjamin: I drive trucks downtown. I agree that King Edward is a bad choice. There is plenty of room running from the Parkway to St. Patrick. It would make more sense for trucks to take it, but the Vanier Parkway is deemed a "no trucks" route. That leaves trucks with no choice but to zigzag through downtown. Trust me, truckers don't want to mess up traffic, but they have no choice.

Vicki: a group called Parks Not Pavement raised over $85,000 to fight the change, which would have saved maybe 20 seconds for each driver. Trucks were never intended for the Vanier Parkway and would have continued to move through downtown. Happily, planning styles and budgets changed and it didn't happen. No matter how hateful it is, having the trucks on King Edward, moving them from one neighbourhood to another was not the answer.

LeRoy: Nevertheless, a Vanier Parkway connection to the 417 would have solved so many congestion problems and been a "simple connection."

Vicki: Let's agree to disagree. Connecting Vanier to the Macdonald-Cartier Bridge would not have solved the truck problem. What we do agree on is there's a problem. King Edward is a horror.

Anneke: Those of us who grew up using the parkland knew the value of it and fought to save it. Yes, there was a railway easement, but while the tracks were there, on either side there was wild parkland, play parks, ballparks, a swimming pool (tragically torn down and replaced with gravel and a few exercise spots) and actual wildlife. The Vanier Parkway was forced on the east end. There were other places that traffic could have been directed, including the site of the Rideau Centre. Instead, the city thought it could bully New Edinburgh into losing its parkland. They failed and people have been whining ever since. Get over it. Use the parks and enjoy them. You can thank us later!

(CANADA SCIENCE AND TECHNOLOGY MUSEUM CN ON-542-9)

Demise of the
Sir John Carling Building

When the Sir John Carling building opened near Dow's Lake in 1967, it was regarded as an architectural jewel.

Alas, the modernist design turned out to be cursed with "sick building syndrome," caused by mold, asbestos, and poor ventilation. Although tons of money was spent on remediation, the building eventually had to come down.

On July 13, 2014, when the building was imploded, I was there with thousands of other people, all ready with my camera on a tripod, cable release in hand.

As the seconds ticked by I grew impatient and turned to my wife to ask her what time it was. As soon as I turned my head, I heard: "Boom, Boom, Boom."

I turned back to press my camera release — only to find my camera had just fallen asleep! By the time it woke up, I had missed the whole thing! Before and after was all I got.

Jeff: Spent a summer there working in the Information Division, splitting time between pamphlet order fulfillment and Experimental Farm tours on an old wagon.

Beverley: I worked in the Information Division in 1970. Building was beautiful then.

(LOST OTTAWA)

Julie: I remember when they built it, as "state of the art." Not that long ago. How did it get to be redundant this soon?

Mike: Having worked there, the building was not maintained well. At least that was my impression.

Phillip: I did some work in this building. It was terrible. Poorly built and ugly. Narrow hallways, poor climate control. For once, I think Public Works did the right thing. A Sir John Carling Park would be better than this crappy building.

Anneke: The building was riddled with problems that included mold and asbestos, and such poor air handling that for decades employees complained of breathing problems and asthma-like symptoms. They had already spent far too much on refurbishments and renovations and the problems were never ameliorated.

Andrew: It's not that great a loss when you consider the asbestos content and its mal-adaptation to technical requirements. It was, like National Defence Headquarters (NDHQ), a brutalist excrescence.

Ted: NDHQ is an ugly box, but this building was quite intriguing. I have never forgotten the public talk I attended in the '60s where Bill Teron praised it as one of the most interesting modernist buildings in town.

Shirley: My grandson Eyrk and great-grandson Peyton (5 years old) got up really early to witness the demolition.

Sherry: I was there with my family – my four-year-old and my eleven-year-old stepdaughter. It was awesome!

Mitchell: I was there, and we had a great view, then it all happened so fast I couldn't get my camera ready either!

Stephanie: Heard the kaboom at 7 a.m. on the dot!

Andrew: Shook the house 5.5 km away in the Golden Triangle.

Diane: We heard it from the Alta Vista area.

Michel: The explosion was very loud. I'm in the Tunney's Pasture area and the explosion made thunder sound like a whisper.

Jan: I wasn't there, but I heard the thunderclap sound of it crashing down. Dramatic.

Aliza: Had toyed with going, but forgot that it was this week ... until I was startled awake by the booms in Old Ottawa South!

Jocelyne: Forgot about this and I thought we had been hit by some kind of bombs ... a bit scary!

Lynda: Slept through. Never heard a thing.

Lunch at the Super Ex

Lunch in Lost Ottawa? How about a hot roast-beef sandwich and fries at the Super Ex in 1988, which was the 100th anniversary of the fair.

Shared by Charlie Stroltzfus, this picture got people remembering the fair, and especially the food. Alas, the fair closed in 2011.

Bonar: I can smell this picture ...

Lee: I can hear the music, the screams from the riders in the distance, the sounds of the guys at the games, trying to lure people in to play. And the smells! Candy apples, popcorn, fries ... ohhhh, the memories!

Penny: I remember the sideshows, the burlesque girls, the motorcycle daredevils, the double Ferris wheel, the Bullet, bingo, and so much more. It was the event to end all summer events. You could spend the day there and come home with all kinds of things! A piece of childhood history gone.

Patricia: How about the house raffle for one dollar? And the draw to win a new car, held every day, using the number on your entry ticket?

Donald: With the new cars elevated on stands around the park and people dreaming of being the lucky winner.

Kim: My first date with my husband was at the Ex. We used to go every year on the same day and get a coin made from the machine with the date on it. Then we had to get chips from the truck right by the Civic Centre, Tiny Tom donuts for dessert, and a candy apple on the way out.

Lise: That candy apple stand on the left belonged to my aunt and uncle. That was always my first and last stop on each visit. Free candy apple and cotton candy!

Joseph: I loved the "hot roast beef on lemonade French fries."

Judy: I miss the bacon sandwiches from the guys with the funny hats. Kiwanis?

Tasha: The Shriners had a food stand near the Cattle Castle. Helped out there one year. They ALSO wore funny hats.

Donald: The Lions Club also sold back bacon on a bun and corn on the cob.

Sharon: Bacon on a bun — my favorite!

Brian: St. Giles Church booth ... the best eats.

Barry: Pogos were first started at the Ex, I think. It was Alex Dayton that started selling them there, a great old Kinsman or Kiwanis gentleman from the Carlingwood area.

Joe: I think Bryan Ferry played the grandstand that year. Great show.

Barry: I worked stage crew at the arena for the Royal Lipizzaner horse show and the Supreme's grandstand show. Saw Karen Carpenter for the last time. Doobie's concert, Chicago, Burton Cummings. Numerous Beach Boy concerts inside, that had the big beams rocking up and down to a scary point. Other big-time concerts too numerous to mention.

Donald: The grandstand shows were not included with Ex admission, but a show ticket did get you into the Ex. There were big name acts like Neil Young, Supertramp, Bob Seger, Pink Floyd.

Patricia: Don't forget Abba.

Marilyn: Roy Rogers and Dale Evans!

Debbie: Those were the days and we are the lucky ones who got to experience it. There's nothing like it now.

Cindy: The music. The food. The Ex was something to look forward to every summer as a kid. Wish my eight year-old son could experience the thrill today.

Patricia: Well, kids today have their cell phones I guess.

Yaghi's Neighborhood Market

(SHARED BY LESLIE JUDEN)

Leslie Juden shared this picture of Yaghi's Mini Mart, a local landmark on Fifth Avenue in the Glebe, across from Mutchmor Public School.

Wrote Leslie: "Yaghi's on Fifth Ave, demolished this week. Ziki Wahab was a really nice guy who ran a great corner store. So many bags of milk bought here and — as a kid going to Mutchmor — a whole lot of candy too!"

A family-run business up to the '90s, succeeding owners just couldn't keep the corner store going.

Brian: So sad to hear that Yaghi's is gone. Does anyone remember the Mello Rolls ice cream, Silverwood's, and three blackballs for a penny?

Linda: I remember Silverwood's and the blackballs and Hawkins potato chips, where you would often find a penny or a nickel taped in the bag!

Charlene: Mello Rolls were the best. Nothing has ever really replaced them. I remember the blackballs had a coriander seed in the centre and coloured layers you couldn't crack. Then there were wax teeth, real licorice pipes, and red wax lips!

Mary: Mello Rolls, that brings back memories of going to Yaghi's after school with just a bit of money. Skating at the outdoor rink on Friday night and sitting in the snow bank with ice cold drinks. Warming up in the shack, which had a real wood stove, and a guy who kept the fire going.

Loretta: I used to fry my gloves on that wood stove in the shack. Best of times!

Fran: I remember the shack. Girls on one side, boys on the other. The rink-men ruled with iron fists!

Ruth: We lived in an apartment on Morris Street until I was almost five. My treat for going to Yaghi's to buy cigarettes for my grandmother was often a Mello Roll. I didn't have to cross the street to get there, so I think I started doing this errand shortly after I learned to walk and talk!

Fran: We lived around the corner on Fourth and loved Yaghi's. Baseball cards, with gum in them, were a favourite.

Matthew: I bought a lot of Star Wars cards and played a lot of Spy Hunter there. I remember as a young kid sounding out "Chocco-Lotto," and Ziki giving me the strangest look. He had no idea what I was trying to say.

Tom: My grandparents lived at 165 Fifth Avenue in the early '60s. I remember walking down Fifth with one of those old plastic milk jugs with the red handle, granddad watching me and letting me know when it was okay to cross the street. I was always able to keep the jug deposit. Which I spent on candy at Yaghi's.

Don: My grandparents lived at Third Avenue and Perry. When we were kids of five and seven years of age, my grandfather would walk us to Yaghi's to get a treat. Ziki would always tease my cousin and I about having girlfriends.

Brian: I remember the lines through the store the first week of school as Mutchmor students went to pick up their free brown-paper book covers. Ads for Walkers bread on them, if I remember correctly. There was a second door on the west side of the building, so the line of students flowed easily out of the store after they got their covers.

Mike: I remember this store when I was a student at Corpus Christi in the early '70s. The smokes came a few years later.

Patricia: Everyone in the Glebe went there and knew these fine people. I also went to Mutchmor across the street. At the time, a new rule was made that none of the children from Corpus Christi or Mutchmor could go to the store during recess. Talk about child abuse. We were all traumatized!

Unveiling of the War Memorial

(LIBRARY AND ARCHIVES CANADA, MIKAN 4090449)

Here's the crowd that gathered in Confederation Square on May 21, 1939, to attend the unveiling of the War Memorial by King George VI and Queen Elizabeth (the Queen Mum). That's the Royal Couple in the car leaving the scene after mixing with the crowd, and shaking the hands of many veterans.

The unveiling was one of a series of hugely popular events that took place in Ottawa during the Royal Visit, which, in hindsight, seems a little sad. The purpose of the Memorial was to honor those who fell in the Great War — the War to End All Wars — but the dedication took place at a time when everyone was more-or-less certain a new war was coming.

That's why the King and Queen were on a month-long tour across Canada, which was the first visit by a reigning monarch. The goal was to drum up support for Mother England, and it succeeded.

I put this photo up on Remembrance Day, less than a month after Corporal Nathan Cirillo was killed while on guard duty at the War Memorial.

Franca: Wow, didn't know there were that many people in Ottawa in 1939.

Margaret: My mother was there, somewhere in that crowd.

Jeff: Apparently there hasn't been a crowd as large as 1939, but today's may break it. Sad, though, that it takes a tragedy to bring people out.

Chris: In fairness, there are a lot more ceremonies around town now.

Jan: I was there today. It was amazing.

Sarah: Amazing to see, and proud to call Ottawa home!

Wanda: Thank you Lost Ottawa for connecting us to our past in such immediate ways.

Streetcars on Sunnyside

This picture of an Ottawa Transportation Commission streetcar making a turn past a Shell Station was originally posted as an Evening Puzzler.

The date seemed to be sometime in the '50s, but the question was — where?

People had the answer, and a few memories to go along with it.

Peter: Looks like the Mayfair Theater in the background, so my guess is Bank and Sunnyside.

Iain: Yes, it's the Mayfair. The Shell station was there until '68.

Bernita: It was a Pioneer in the '90s.

Ray: I pumped gas at that corner in the late '60s. Gas was 39 cents a gallon.

Marnie: I knew those buildings and that was a beautiful Shell station.

Max: Is that a White Hen down the road?

Richard: Not a White Hen, but a White Rose station!

Charles: White Rose gasoline. Company was bought out by Shell, as it happens.

Stewart: According to my father (Bruce Dudley, OTC Operator 697 in the '50s), the streetcar is southbound on Bank, and turning west on Sunnyside Ave. It will do a big rectangle, from Sunnyside to Seneca, Seneca to Grove, and Grove to Bank, which was the end of the Bank Line. When it was time to go, he turned north on Bank and came up the grade to Sunnyside on the tracks you can see in the foreground.

Brian: That's right, the streetcar is turning west from Bank Street onto Sunnyside, and it was the best line to bunk because it was downhill to Grosvenor!

Marilyn: I was born and raised in Ottawa South on Rosedale Avenue and rode the "Bank Street Bullet" many times in my 16 years there.

Karina: I grew up near there and never knew there had been a streetcar! Very cool.

Charles: I can remember the streetcar turnaround, a block or two south. My mom and I used to walk there and take the streetcar downtown to see a movie.

Jennifer: I went to the Mayfair every Saturday as a kid to spend my big allowance of 35 cents.

Charmion: The Rexall sign is for Coulter's Drugstore.

Scott: My mother's hair salon was beside Coulter's Drugs. All the bad kids from Hopewell used to smoke beside the theatre.

Patricia: I remember there was a tobacco store to the left of the theatre entrance.

Tom: My dad grew up in this neighborhood and got what was probably his first job in the drugstore, along with a friendship that lasted years. He got my birthday present one year from Coulter's, where he used to stop in on his way home after work, going in by the back door on Sunnyside. One day he walked into the back, where the druggists were. Mr. Coulter (or maybe his son), had found a beagle dog — and that became my first dog, Mutt.

Suzanne: I remember the Ottawa Public Library across the street. It was my first introduction to the library system, circa 1965, and it cost ten cents to get a card!

Ryan: I used to live at 223 Sunnyside in a big, old red brick house. It was thought to be the first house built in Old Ottawa South, sometime around 1860. My landlady had an old picture of the place and all you could see was fields, all the way down to the Rideau River. Pretty cool.

Margaret: We drove by this intersection every Sunday on the way from Billings Bridge to church. Riverside was then a dirt road to the city dump and it flooded every spring.

Judy: It was great growing up in Old Ottawa South. Of course, it was just Ottawa South at the time. I guess the "old" part was bound to happen.

Waiting for the Train

December 30, 2014: 241 likes, 55 shares, 40 comments and 8,104 reached

Every once in a while we come across a picture that has never been seen before, like this shot of travelers in the waiting hall of Ottawa's Union Station in 1954.

The waiting hall is a magnificent space that hasn't been used for train travel since the station was closed in 1966. It's a decision that most people now find regrettable, but pictures of the station still transport them back in time.

(CANADA SCIENCE AND TECHNOLOGY MUSEUM CN-49845-7)

Bob: This was my first impression of Ottawa when I arrived from Scotland in '66.

Tasha: This is where I made my "grand entrance" into the city. I just wish I could remember more than a lady with a scary stole around her neck.

Deb: I was there a lot when I was a little girl. I remember how it felt when I looked up. Sooooo big!

Carol: So classy!

Don: Any wonder travel by train has an enduring appeal to so many?

Arnold: I love trains and old train stations. It was a great way to travel — especially the bar car and dining car.

Michael: I loved this train station! Said goodbye to some good friends there. Memories! Tears, too, as a little kid.

Max: Is it all marble?

Andrew: The interior is plaster. Walls, columns and ceiling. Only the floor is marble. The ceiling isn't self-supporting, but rather plaster suspended from a steel frame hidden above. This and the Chateau Laurier are two early Ottawa examples of steel-frame construction, with all the interior and exterior masonry (real stone and fake) just for show.

Francine: I used to go there every Saturday to watch the trains come in. Then I would head over to Freiman's to get my malted milk, then walk back to Hull via the Interprovincial Bridge.

Carole: I did the same thing, but took the bus back to Hull. Just loved those malted milks. If anyone knows where to get some, please let me know!

Michael: OMG, malted milk. At two for five cents or one for ten cents. My cousin measured them, and two for five cents had more.

Carolyne: They had decks of cards available for people waiting. As pre-teens, my sister and I used to go to the station just to play a game of rummy in the tunnel to the Chateau Laurier.

Margo: I remember taking the tunnel over to the Chateau. We would go swimming there and eat at the cafeteria. Memories!

Diane: Remember the Honey Dew restaurant next door to the train station? We used to go to the station, cross over to the Chateau through the tunnel, then cross the street again for an orange drink and a hot dog!

Dave: When I was first posted from my trade's training to C.F.S. Carp, I arrived here late Sunday night and slept on one of those benches until Monday morning, when I went to the temporary buildings and was whisked off to the Hole. That began a love affair with Carp that remains to this day.

Carol: My dad was an engineer for CN and sometimes we used to pick him up at the station after a run. Beautiful architecture! If the city had been smart, this would have remained the train station.

Christine: This is the building Ottawa should have used for the rail system they are building now. It would have made good use of a historical building. They could have put businesses inside like New York's Union Station, thereby enticing tourists to visit another Ottawa landmark, creating more revenue for the city. The building has been wasted as a Conference Centre.

Betty: I remember this station, and agree. It should have been kept in service.

Paul: Atlas Shrugged?

Typing Class at Laurentian High School

August 19, 2014: 217 likes, 69 shares, 77 comments and 7,788 reached

Typing class at Ottawa's Laurentian High School in 1959. By Jove, there are even some guys in the back there!

Kidding aside, I wish I had taken typing class. I do it all day long, like everyone else, but I'm still pretty bad at it.

My biggest problem is that I never learned how to use the shift keys properly for capital letters. Do they even have typing class any more? Never too late to learn?

This was Lost Ottawa's most popular post in 2014.

Clifford: I took typing in high school because the class was full of girls!

Norma: It's called "keyboarding" now.

Steve: I am under the impression that they teach "keyboarding" instead of cursive, which is going to lead to trouble in the future. If you don't know cursive, how are you going to be able to read old handwritten documents?

Rolande: It will become ancient script. Like hieroglyphics. You'll have to take a special class in archaeology.

Marilyn: My father said he would only make us do two things: learn to swim and learn to type. Both have been invaluable.

Judy: My mother made me take typing in Grade 11 and I was stuck with a bunch of Grade 9 students. The horror! But as you say, learning typing skills has been invaluable. The "learn to swim" is still on my bucket list!

Aliza: My mother made me take typing too — two weeks of summer school at a secretarial college when I was between Grade 7 and 8 (she wanted it to be before I had to do a lot of typing for school, and thus wouldn't get stuck in bad habits). They had no idea what to do with a 12 year old, but it worked. I learned to touch type, and type fast, and I didn't have to waste a high school elective credit on typing. Instead, I was able to take computer programming (in the late '80s).

David: I had a choice between typing and conversational French. I thought: "I'm in a bilingual country, and why would I need to type?" A few years later I got into computers, and a few years after that moved to the States. So much for career planning, although I am one of the fastest "three-finger" typists ever seen!

Anna: I wonder if that is Mrs. Bullman's class at Laurentian. She was the typing teacher there for years and taught me to type in the late '60s.

Paula: I think I took typing one year in that very same classroom! It breaks my heart to think that Laurentian High School became a Walmart.

Alison: This is neat! I took a typing class at Laurentian High School in '89. Actually, I took it twice! My husband is quite impressed with my typing skills now though, and I owe it all to this class. He likes it when he has something to say to me, and I turn to look at him, but keep typing while he's talking.

Michael: I took two years of typing class at Laurentian. The essentials of good posture and proper hand position were reinforced daily with the occasional tap on the back of the wrist by our teacher's wooden pointer.

James: I took typing at Woodroffe High School. The teacher told me that if I promised not to take typing again next year she would pass me!

Isabel: I was at Ridgemont in '63 and my electives were typing and Latin! Go figure. Both of them have stood me in good stead all these years! Those great big Remingtons with blank keys. I'll never forget them (nor poor Mr. Farmer, our Latin teacher).

Debbie: I remember those Ridgemont days, with the picture of the typing keyboard at the front on the chalkboard. I just loved typing class and did really well in it. I ended up being a secretary for many years and loved that too.

Judy: I was at Ridgemont for 1967-70, I think. Mr. Greatrex was our teacher. Loved typing. Glad I took it. Even taught my son, who was grateful when he went into computers. No two-finger typing for him!

Julie: I was at Ridgemont in '62, and think we must have looked like the kids in the picture, typing to "Turkey in the Straw" and other classics. Then, when we got really good: "The quick brown fox jumped over the lazy dog." I think I still hear music in the background when I'm typing ... long live those great days of learning the keystrokes to music!

Dorothy: Wasn't it "the lazy sleeping dog"?

Scott: "The quick brown fox jumped over the lazy dog's back."

Helen: I took typing back when computers and even electric typewriters were in the future. I remember, "The quick brown fox jumped over the very lazy dog." And "The man and the boy got the day off, but got the pay for it." From the late-'60s. No spellcheck in those days.

Carole: Typing class was pretty standard for everyone back in the '50s. I remember typing: "Now is the time for all good men to come to the aid of their country!"

Dawn: I learned to type in the late '70s at Almonte and District High School. My teacher's name was Mrs. Lamb and her favourite expression was "Hands on Home Keys."

Kellie: I was at Sir Wilfrid Laurier. I can still hear my typing teacher (gosh I can't remember his name but he reminded me of Big Bird) chanting out ASDFJKL semi-colon RETURN THE CARRIAGE! Good times!

Vince: I remember it well from Glebe Collegiate.... "juj space, juj, space", a zillion times with the typing teacher, the delectable Miss Usher. But who knew I'd go into information technology as a computer programmer and business analyst and the keyboard would be a huge part of my life. I type like the wind.

Helen: I remember learning to type with blank keys. It was the only way to learn how to touch type, but I'm glad I have those letters now ... and this new thing called spellcheck.

Ron: I have been on the One Finger Hunch and Punch method for years. You can get pretty good at it.

Al: I never did learn how to use the eight other digits on my hands.

Diane: I took typing at Fisher Park High in '59 with Mr. Piche. But, look at me now, I type with two thumbs on my I-pad.

2015

Charlie's Diner

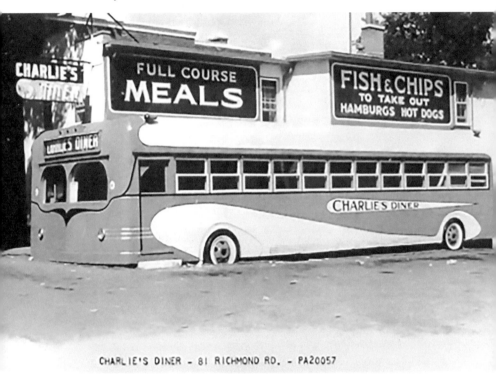

CHARLIE'S DINER - 81 RICHMOND RD. - PA20057

Charlie's Diner, at 81 Richmond Road, circa 1945. Now the site of Napoli Pizza, just past Island Park.

You don't get many opportunities to eat at establishments like this anymore. A classic.

Linda: The restaurant was started by my grandfather. Then my dad and uncle ran it. I lived upstairs, along with my sibs Larry, Paul, and Christine. So many memories! The photo is a copy of a postcard Grandpa LeDuc had made. Note the address and the phone number. "PA" stood for Parkway.

Denise: I stayed upstairs with Peggy and her family many times. Peggy and I went to Jeanne D'Arc convent together. I loved going over there as we could get milkshakes anytime. And they were fabulous!

Dave: I remember my dad was a friend with the two brothers. When I was small, I would play upstairs.

Mario: My mother worked there from 1967 to '70.

Linda: Mario, your mom was Ursula? If so, I remember her as a kind and lovely lady. My dad said that she was a great person, then laughed and explained that he drove her home one night and she invited him in for an espresso. It was the first he ever had, and he felt his like his head would explode!

Kim: I can remember stopping in with granny and grandpa (Marge and Don) Shouldice to visit with your parents and Moe and Eddy. Always a friendly place.

Ray: I would stop in sometimes after delivering my newspapers. The food was always great.

Bruce: Ate in the diner with my mother when I was a wee lad.

Bram: I had lunch there a few times with my dad, who worked nearby at the Canadian Bank Note.

Susan: My husband and I had our first date there!

Judy: I ate there many times, west of Island Park, just down the street from the Dew Drop Inn.

Jeff: I walked past Charlie's and the Dew Drop Inn many times, on my way to Hilson Public School from our house on Patricia.

Brenda: I went to Hilson and walked by Charlie's Diner all the time. Brings back good childhood memories.

Donna: I walked by that diner every day on my way to Hilson. I even went in a few times to buy penny candies they kept at the front counter.

Diana: I grew up in Westboro and remember the diner. I also remember buying ice cream cones for seven cents at the Dominion grocery (now the site of MEC). The ice cream came tube-shaped, wrapped in paper, and was unwrapped and placed in the cone.

Beverley: Those were called Mello Rolls. The year they increased the price to 10 cents, we protested for at least a week.

Janet: Did you sit inside the bus to eat?

Beverley: Yes. There was a complete restaurant inside.

Mary: I passed the old bus countless times on the way to the cottage at Shirley's Bay in the '50s.

Ross: Drove by it hundreds of time with mom and dad when I was a kid, but never got to go in. Too close to home, I guess, since we lived on Roosevelt Ave. Boy it brings back memories.

Myra: Born and raised in Ottawa. Saw the diner many times but never ventured in ... my loss.

End of the World

An Ottawa Transportation Commission bus at the corner of Broadview and Carling, circa 1952.

Shared by Dave Alston, the picture seems rather unremarkable – but it generated so much interest it ended up being the third most popular picture on Lost Ottawa in 2015.

Eric: Holy crap! It was country back then! Well before my time!

Genny: Hard to even imagine that this was the far west end at one point!

Carla: The boonies.

Toon: The bus looks like it's at the end of the world. The change in the landscape today is amazing. I imagine people will say the same thing about the Orleans/Kanata/Barrhaven fringes in 40 years, if we let the sprawl continue.

Aliza: I was just at that corner this morning for a doctor's appointment and thinking how much the city had grown since I went to one of the schools around the corner. And also thinking about how ugly that stretch of Carling is now!

Shereen: I remember that field! Coldest walk ever walking up to Nepean High ... Brrrr.

Ken: I got a nail in my heel walking through it when the Red Barn was there. I too am a former Nepean alumnus. Go Knights!

Peter: I walked in the other direction to St. Basil's and later St. Joe's high school.

Anna: Wow! I went to Notre Dame High School right at this corner. It's so interesting to see how different it once looked.

Fred: Lady Jane doughnuts used to be at Carling and Broadview when I worked at A&P in the '70s. I believe it's now a Pizza Pizza.

Kirsten: Wow, that's a name I haven't heard in a while. Hung out at Lady Jane's before it closed.

Elizabeth: Red Barn on one corner. Lady Jane on the other.

Connie: Brenda Lancaster and I got food poisoning at Lady Jane's Doughnuts. She would like the fact that there's a bus in this photo – considering she threw up inside one on the way home!

Carmen: Time has changed so much. I remember stopping at Lady Jane Doughnuts before visiting my doctor across the street on Broadview. Many fond memories.

Cathie: Great shot. There are a few houses in the background, built on a golf course. Our house was built in 1952 on the 9th hole, or so I was always told.

Melissa: And in the distance you can see Dovercourt Avenue!

Sharon: That's where the medical building and high school are located now.

Adele: I lived at the corner of Carling and Maitland for many years and remember this big empty field on Broadview.

Steven: That's right, the field beyond the bus was a swamp where kids would go to hide out and smoke.

Jim: Looks like the bus is sliding a bit. Wonder what the make was, a Flexible? Not a GM coach.

Bruce: Looks like a 320 Faegol Twin Coach, the first bus I drove after my training in '57.

Matthieu: Old-school baby!

Liz: I remember those buses. What can I say? Another generation.

Melody: I think I caught that bus last week.

The Rocket Goes Up
at Science and Tech

Here's the Atlas rocket arriving at the Science and Technology Museum on St. Laurent Boulevard, August 31, 1973. That's the day the "Rocket," as everyone called it, was installed in Technology Park.

Once used to power ICBMs, Atlas rockets were also used to boost early US astronauts into space, and that's why this one was brought to Ottawa. The Museum had a huge space exhibit on the floor at the time.

The Rocket stood there as an iconic landmark for more than 40 years, but unbeknownst to most people it couldn't really stand up by itself. To remain stiff, it had to be inflated with compressed air.

Between compressor failures and holes developing in the thin metal skin, it was decided to take the Rocket down before it fell down. This item was posted just after the removal was announced.

Barry: I was working for a security firm as dispatcher and got a call at nine a.m. from the United States telling me to have ten guards at the border the following morning. They were delivering a rocket. Well, OK! We escorted it to the museum. It was quite an event at the time.

Melanie: And now it's being taken away. Another loss.

Hans: So sad to see it go.

Steve: It's about dollars and cents, unfortunately, and no one has enough of it to commit to restoring, repairing or preserving this piece of history.

Thomas: If it was worth acquiring, it is worth preserving. Not everything government or its agencies does has to be cost effective.

Bill: Restore it!

Robert: If its needs a home, I'll take it and look after it.

Deborah: They're taking it down, because there is a chance it will fall down.

Jeff: I wish they would take a moment and think of the historical nature of this item for space exploration, science, and Ottawa itself. They could find a way to mount it horizontally, like they've done at museums in the US for decades. Losing this is a mistake.

Kris: Lay it on its side like it was on the trailer in this picture and keep it for the future. If absolutely necessary, fill it with foam to preserve it, although I'd like to see the inside.

Carolyn: Why not just buy a new compressor for it?

Steve: According to a gentleman interviewed on the radio, it's not so much a fault with compressors, but the shell of the rocket itself that is developing increasingly larger leaks and can't be sustained any longer.

David: Science and Technology? Nobody in the government "brain trust" could figure out a fix? Oh! I forgot for a moment we are talking about Ottawa!

Andy: The rocket has been there for as long as I can remember. I grew up in Alta Vista, worked for years at the Esso at the end of Othello, and visited the museum all the time as a kid. That super-cool and shiny rocket was always there.

Peter: I remember as a kid, it was always explained as an amazing rocket connected to the space program. As I got older I learned it was also used as an ICBM, with nuclear warheads.

Jeff: Kids love going to the museum, and even if the rocket is gone, I'll always bring it up anytime we drive by. Sometimes things have to change, but they don't have to be forgotten!

Luis: Still, the end of an era.

Joe: Gotta make room for condos!

(CANADA SCIENCE ADN TECHNOLOGY MUSEUM 73-16564)

The Rocket Comes Down

And then it was gone. The day of this post was the day The Rocket was removed from the front lawn of Science and Tech.

Although people had known for nearly two weeks about the decision to remove the Rocket — our second post about the Rocket's demise got more comments than our first.

Shawn: No!

Lea: Gasp.

Peggy: That was the only way I could find the place. So sad!

Suzanne: One more for Lost Ottawa.

Sandra: Wow. I can't believe they removed it.

Nancy: End of an era.

Shawn: Do another step backwards Ottawa. Slow clap.

Stephane: Sigh. What's next to go, the lighthouse?

Dave: As long as the crazy kitchen is safe, I'm almost prepared to let this slide.

Matt: Get rid of the crazy kitchen. We don't need fun things there!

Lorne: My father-in-law was monumental in putting up this rocket many years ago. Fondly known as the Bic Pen by the family. To Bud Wickware and the rocket ... R.I.P.

Chris: I vividly remember this from growing up. I went to Skateway across the street and the Video Warehouse next door to play free Atari games.

Geoffrey: That totally sucks. Every time I visit home, something from my childhood is gone.

Carolyn: When they have to cut it up, they should make little spaceship shapes and sell them!

Liz: Good idea. Auction off the pieces as part of Ottawa history.

Allen: I'd buy a piece.

Marta: It is such a shame to see these things being lost. I have to wonder why there was no preventative maintenance for this, or the entire museum for that matter. Sad.

Jonathan: It could have been placed on its side in the Aviation Museum. To cut it up is a waste of a good relic.

David: It's not up to the museum. The rocket is owned by the US Navy, and they specifically said if it comes down it must be destroyed, so no one can study how it was made.

Jonathan: The museum is in control of the rocket's status as a display piece. The Aviation Museum is part of the same corporation as the Science Museum. I suggest that an attempt could have been made to save it for continued horizontal, indoor display.

Rob: Sad to let something so spectacular deteriorate. As someone said, the museum was originally a bakery (actually, it was supposed to be a bakery distribution centre — Ed.) Why the hell can't the government spend money properly and build an appropriate science and technology center of world-class status? (It has now! — Ed.)

Toon: Our team submitted an RFP to the museum with a vision for something amazing (sustainable, exciting, sponsored, linked to museums and research centres) but found out today that we didn't even make the first cut. Proof the place has no vision.

Mitch: More childhood memories gone, due to poor management.

Robert: It is supposed to be sent for salvage, as the US doesn't want it back. I told them they could have brought it to me and I'd set it over top a concrete silo in my pasture.

Mike: It just never got off the ground.

(LOST OTTAWA)

Ronald's Caboose

In 1981, the Science and Tech Museum put up the lighthouse that still stands at the corner of St. Laurent and Lancaster Road.

Who wouldn't want to take a photo from the top of it? This photo shows the McDonald's at St. Laurent and Bourassa, which then had Ronald's Caboose out back.

Julie: I had my birthday party in that caboose!

Philip: I had one birthday in that caboose. I think it was number five.

Daniel: I had two birthdays there.

Hugh: I had three birthday parties in the caboose. Every second year, I'd be begging my parents!

Blayne: I had a few birthdays there. For my ninth, we had to share it with a girls' party. We ended up in a huge food fight. Burgers and fries everywhere.

Shawn: Having your birthday party in the caboose was the mark of a "cool kid." My birthdays number 5 and 8 were in the caboose, so I guess I was only cool every three years or so.

Pat: I was a hostess for birthday parties in that caboose!

Kathy: I worked at that McDonalds and did many parties as a hostess … great memories.

Jennifer: The caboose is where we had our management meetings … leaky, stinky and cold!

Lori: I worked at that McDonald's in the '80s. I remember "Bus Season," countless parties with the crew, and many breakfast shifts where the whole crew had hangovers from the night before.

Wes: Remember the table near the top of the caboose with the ladder to get to it?

Alexander: I remember that old caboose. Whatever happened to it?

Robert: The caboose is on an orchard farm, just outside of Balderson near Perth. The guy bought it for $10,000. I did a delivery there once, and the guy let me go and take a look. It was a lot smaller than I remember. That section in the middle that you had to climb up was only shoulder height. I guess when you're little everything seems much bigger. Fun times!

Carol: The McDonald's in Bells Corners used to have a caboose too. It also had the original Golden Arches sign where the "M" started on the ground.

Wes: The caboose from Bells Corners was turned into a chip wagon on Main Street in Stittsville in the late '90s. No clue where it is now.

Paul: The first McDonalds to open, I believe, was in '68 or '69 on Merivale Road at Family Brown. A burger, a coke and fries for less than a buck. I loved it ... until the Red Barn came to town.

Tom: That McDonald's on Merivale opened in '69. A young lady living in a house full of stoner degenerates, where I too resided, worked graveyard there. We would marshal a ride home for her at closing. She'd often bring leftovers and BAGS of burgers. No Big Macs!

Allen: Ottawa's first Burger King was across the street from this one on St. Laurent.

Christian: Also the first Tim Horton's in the east end, right next door to the Burger King.

Ted: And Skyline Cable Vision.

Donna: We used to pile into this McDonald's every Saturday night after roller skating at the Skadium on Lancaster. We would hit up the Burger King across the street after the all-nighters, because McD's was not open for breakfast back then.

Michel: Why was the caboose removed? Seems it was pretty popular.

Jennifer: Today they would likely have to license such a venue for it to be successful. "Yes, McPinot, please."

The British Hotel

(CITY OF OTTAWA ARCHIVES CA004651)

The British Hotel in Aylmer was a favorite watering hole for folks from Ottawa back in the day, when drinking laws were considerably different on both sides of the river.

It looks so nice here, in the '50s, and has been thoroughly renovated since, but it was once famous for being very rough. You could expect a fight at any time — but, hey, you could also drink until three in the morning!

Shared by Anneke Dubash, from the City of Ottawa Archives.

Tasha: So that's what it looked like in the daylight.

Gary: Never seen it with sunshine!

Darlene: This picture makes it nicer than it really was, believe me.

Anne: First place in Quebec as a kid that I went to drink! I've heard the British has been restored as a heritage building and will be re-opening soon. I can't wait!

Christine: The British and the Chaudiere were the places to be on Friday and Saturday nights in the '70s and early '80s. Live bands, cheap beer (quarts!), and under-age drinking. I think I was 15 the first time I got served at the Chaud.

Peter: The "A", "B", and "C" of Aylmer nightlife: the Alymer, the British and the Chamberlain hotels.

Wayne: In the early '60s it was the Ottawa House (Ronnie Hawkins & The Hawks) the Chaud and the British Hotel. Many good times, indeed.

Dorothy: The British was just up the street from my family's home in Aylmer (1889-1946). My great uncle took dancing lessons there for 50 cents a lesson.

Derek: That's where I met my wife for the first time, at the British.

Philip: That's where I lost my wife.

Doug: We would go there to see Major Hoople's Boarding House in the late '60s. The bar was definitely dumpier than the picture.

Louise: My mom and dad played music there in the mid-'40s and '50s. My dad was a fiddler. My mom had a voice like Kitty Wells and played the standup bass. When Hughie Scott was a teenager, they would let him up to sing a few Elvis tunes. Their stage names were Tony and Lucille King.

Cheryl: I hung out there awhile, when it was really rough.

Donald: Lots of fights!

Eric: Lots of bloodstains on the wall!

Bruce: Friday Nights ... Beers and a Brawl!

Gary: Last time I was there I was with my wife, when we were still dating. We left right after gunshots from the bathroom.

Bob: Spent many nights partying there, both as a patron, and as a band member. Yeah, it was rough and kinda scuzzy, with brawls where guys threw tables at each other and usually took out the whole room, but man, those were good times.

Michel: I was at the British one night and there was this guy I'd been to D'arcy McGee High School with, walking around bullying people. Eventually he started a fight with a guy who had done nothing more than ask to be left alone. He was really messing up this poor guy's face. I asked the bartender why there wasn't a bouncer to stop it. The bartender said: "That is the bouncer."

The Milk Man in Overbrook

An Ottawa milkman faces a challenge on Prince Albert Street, in Overbrook, May of 1955.

The housing projects along Prince Albert were still new at the time and flooding from the Rideau River was also common in the neighbourhood.

Cathy: My old street! We moved there in '59 ... I guess the roadwork was done by then!

Shirley: I lived on Queen Mary and later on Presland Street. The oldest of five kids. Got hit by a car while sledding toward Tremblay Road (where the old railway tracks were.) I had my best years there.

Claudette: My husband lived on this street way back when. Just put a paved road and more of the same houses ... and voila we're in 2015 as though nothing has changed.

(CITY OF OTTAWA ARCHIVES CA033801)

Ray: Lived at 224. We used to dam the ditch in the spring for fun, and even though the drainage was better, we could still flood the paved street.

Wendy: Still looks like this picture when it rains today! All the streets in Overbrook need to be re-paved.

Brian: My old street ... it flooded during my time there, too.

Joanne: The houses looked the same in 1990 — without the water. Great memories.

Michael: Great photo of the milkman era! Without the horses and their feedbags. Prince Albert was quite a challenging street, I guess!

Grant: What's a milkman?

Salvo: What's he got there besides the milk?

Diane: I think he has a brick of butter and a carton of eggs.

Ron: He's usually got jersey, homo, pasteurized, butter, eggs and cream.

Nancy: I remember milk being delivered in bottles with the cream at the top.

Marnie: I remember the milkman delivering eggs, butter, cream and milk, right to the door.

Laura: Everyone left payment in empty bottles overnight on their front porches. Can't imagine doing that now. At Christmas, my mom always gave him a bonus with a box of chocolates. Makes me smile, seeing this picture.

Jill: This is where we lived (and also the year that I was born). When I was growing up, a visit from the milkman and the bread man was a very happy event, especially when I could talk my mom into the white powder donuts.

Dave: I was one of those milkmen!

Kathy: Fond memories from 314 Prince Albert. My mom would give me 10 cents every day, and I would run up to the truck and get a chocolate milk.

Brian: We couldn't wait for Saturday mornings, once a month, when my mom would get a quart of chocolate milk at the door, followed shortly by the bread man with various pastries. Remember having to mix the two portions to get your butter?

Doreen: We lived at 224 Prince Albert from '59 until '71. I am quite sure I remember this milkman.

Sue: My mother always told me I was the milkman's kid because I was the only one in our family born with red hair!

Hillcrest High School

Up in the morning and off to ... Hillcrest High School, on Dauphin Road, just off Smyth Road between Alta Vista and St. Laurent.

Some lucky student, or maybe a teacher, has a fine British sport cars parked out front, which would seem to date this photo to the decade after the school opened, in 1961.

Laureen: Hey, that's my high school! And yes, I think that's my teacher's car. I forget his name. He got married a few years later and drove a VW Bug!

Bonnie: Might have been Miss Silver's car (the science teacher.)

Laureen: Did Miss Silver have a sports car? I thought it was the commercial teacher. Oh no, he had a T-Bird!

Huss: Looks like an Austin Healey, so this must be early '60s.

Brian: That looks like an Austin Healy to me as well. My neighbor actually owned one. Very cool looking, with a 6-pack carburetor — but I never saw his actually running.

Don: I can't remember any student driving a Healy of that vintage. A rusted out Morris would be more likely!

Bill: Garage door on the right is to the auto shop.

Sharron: I attended Hillcrest in '64, before moving to the west end. Learned to skateboard on that incline in front of the auto shop door. That was before venturing downtown on the bus with friends to hit the path that went down to the canal, where the NAC is now. You would have to wait 10 minutes in line to use that much-favored skateboard incline!

Sharon: Went there from Grade 10 to 13 and graduated in '66. I also learned to skateboard on that hill.

Sandra: Started there in Grade 9, the very day it opened! Wonderful school, amazing education! Graduated '66!

Anne: There were so many students at the school by year two all the large "gathering areas" had become classrooms.

Malcolm: And by 1965-69 they already had portables.

Stephen: My years were 1971-76. The combination of academic, technical and social skills I learned there has been priceless to me in later life. Math, auto mechanics, English, woodwork, history, electrics

(BBROYGBVGW), science, drafting, geography, gym and, perhaps equally important — no political correctness. It was a real school back then, with real people learning real things. The teachers were tough, and rightly so considering that many of us had attitude. Lots of cigarettes, vodka, beer and pot. Did we ever get smashed during football games! Good times, long gone. I feel sorry for kids growing up today in a sterile, paternalistic, hyper-protective environment. They don't stand a chance when they hit the real world.

Bill: Mr. Slater and Mr. Harvey, et al, needed to "counsel" me on a couple of occasions for my miscreant behaviour. The '76 football final springs to mind rather vividly.

John: In '85 I cut my middle finger off in woodshop class at Hillcrest. Stupid key rack.

Mary: Having never seen Hillcrest, I had no idea how similar it looked to my high school, which was Woodroffe.

Bill: Hillcrest was a very typical school for its era, cookie-cutter design that was modified a little for different sites. The bottom line was that it was the students and teachers who made it come alive and relevant to our community.

Chris: Great school, great times!

Donna: Great school and great teachers.

The Willson Mill at Meech Lake

Lac Meech in Gatineau Park is about a half-hour drive from downtown Ottawa. A thirty-minute walk from the south end of the lake will bring you to the ruins of this mill, built in the middle of the forest by Thomas "Carbide" Willson.

It's quite a site, with a broken-down upstream dam, the base of an acid tower, abandoned mill and generating station, and a waterfall. The mill appears to have been built in 1911-12. Now it's a ruin, but it makes for a great Lost Ottawa outing.

In our original post we had several pictures, and a video of the waterfall.

The trail to the ruins is well marked and the bugs weren't too bad when I went. Do wear sensible shoes! I found an abandoned pair of high heels at the site. Apparently, the lady decided it was wiser to walk back in bare feet.

(LOST OTTAWA)

Sam: The Meech Lake Ruins! My favorite place in and around the city!

Pierre: I just love to walk by those ruins!

Peter: I went there with the St. Matthews cub pack when I was a kid!

Dianne: Unbelievable pictures. Almost magical. Looking to take some pictures there in the fall.

Steve: All seems a bit Blair Witchy to me.

Nancy: I have lived in the Ottawa area my whole life and hiked in the Gatineau Hills hundreds of times. I had no idea this was there. Can't wait to find it!

Jaan: This small plant fell into ruin shortly after it was built. It was never intended to be more than a small-scale demonstration of Willson's new process for making chemical fertilizer using hydroelectric power – to be implemented for real on the Saguenay River. Neither Willson nor his partner, William Chisolm, had enough money for the project, so American Tobacco giant J.B. Duke bought in. After an initial meeting with Willson in Ottawa in 1912, a new demonstration plant was set up in Charlotte, NC, where Chisolm's Interstate Chemical had a fertilizer factory and Duke had a large hydroelectric power plant. It is not clear to what extent the Meech Lake pilot project served its purpose of convincing investors. In any case, by 1914, Duke owned everything and Willson was broke. He died in 1915.

Wynn: Gravity affects water, buildings and capital equally, it seems.

Malkolm: I love to photograph this place!

Kevin: The mill is a nudist hangout, or used to be, so don't be shocked if you see a bunch of naked people around. They aren't fans of people taking pictures.

Ray: It was great for nude sunbathing. Wonderful!

Ted: It was once (early-'80s) an official NCC-accepted naturist beach. Then some people complained that it was shocking to passers-by, especially kids, and the NCC retreated. It was widely covered in newspapers at the time.

Mo: An exhibitionist spoiled it for everyone.

George: The NCC has been charging people for nudity the past few years, and at the beach, too, although I'm sure some people still take their chances.

Ian: We discovered that it was "clothing optional" around '72 and got a guided tour through the swimming holes from "Harry the Tour Guide" He tried to convince us to get all-over tans. Unsuccessfully.

Pascal Hardware

July 16, 2015: 687 likes, 192 shares, 203 comments and 37,873 reached

Pascal Hardware, not long after it opened in 1968, in what was then a new shopping plaza on the northeast corner of Merivale and Meadowlands.

Outside, the store was famous for art made from all sorts of rusted metal parts, situated on either side of the entrance. Inside, it was famous for having — everything.

Pascal originally shared the plaza with a Miracle Mart and Steinberg's. All eventually went bankrupt (Pascal in 1991) and there has been a seemingly endless succession of stores since.

Rick: I loved the metal art on the front.

Tony: I spent many an hour looking at the "steel people" on the walls.

Maureen: The wall-art had a bull skull made of metal that used to fascinate me.

Pierre: They also had a giant robot statue. A big tin-man made out of nuts and bolts.

Diane: I went there with my dad all the time in the '70s. Anyone remember the kids' train ride thing they had there at the front of the store, with the big traffic light standard?

Kim: I do! I would ask for money to ride the little train at the front, and always rode it first, whenever we went into the store. Soooo fun!

Dominique: I remember my dad taking us. I would play with the wall of doorbells, check out the anvils, and wonder how the hell Bugs Bunny managed to lift one and drop it on the Road Runner!

Garth: My dad would ask: "who wants to go to Pascal?" We would go and then walk up and down every aisle.

Patti: One of my fondest memories is driving from Manor Park with my grandfather and spending the morning in the store, eating a bagged lunch in the parking lot, then going back into the store for the afternoon!

Vic: Remember the nuts and bolts counter in the centre of the store? The guy behind the counter would help you with the appropriate screw/bolt choices, then sell you as many or as few as you required. Even if it was just one.

Tom: Yes, and I was probably the guy who counted them out first and put them in those little paper bags. Pascal was my first full-time job when I got out of high school in '71.

Chris: Bought my first drafting set there. I still have it.

Leo: That's where I got all my hockey gear. Pascal was the best!

Elizabeth: I bought my first piece of furniture there for my first apartment. It was a dresser and it cost $105. My dad just about choked on the price, since I was only making about $600/month. But I still have that dresser 41 years later!

Lynne: I got my first fishing rod at Pascal, with my dad, when I was about seven or eight.

Tony: I got my first bike there.

Stephanie: I still use the knives I bought there.

Marilyn: We went to buy a BBQ starter for my soon-to-be husband's boss. Romance?

Dave: So tell me, has Merivale always been a terrible street?

Terry: No. At one point it was just a country road. But today it's a commercial street like many across the region. No better or worse.

Tom: We used to ride horses in the fields before it became Parkwood Hills and we used to always take the back roads to get to muddy, pot-holed Merivale Road, risking our lives, especially when big tankers and transports drove past us from the fuel tanks way down Merivale. We rode there to get to Norel Hobbies, Dairy Queen and CJOH TV.

(SHARED BY KLAUS GERKEN)

The Green Valley Christmas Tree

The Christmas tree at the Green Valley Restaurant on Prince of Wales Drive. Shared by former Green Valley owner John Myers.

The tree was a famous landmark in its day, done up by the Green Valley for decades. The tree actually survived the burning of the restaurant in 2003, but not the re-development of the area.

Tammy: I grew up in that area and saw that tree on a daily basis. Loved it when it was lit up at Christmas! So many things and places have changed.

Sharon: My parents had their wedding reception at the Green Valley in '54. I always looked forward to seeing the Christmas tree lit up. A missed landmark for sure!

Louise: I went with a group of photography friends to take pictures before the tree came down. I lay down under it, and took pictures looking up. It was beautiful. Not everyone can appreciate the value of a natural thing.

Ellen: Always loved seeing that tree lit up.

Elena: It brings back lots of good memories. I worked there for 21 years.

Amie: My grandmother, Myrtle Eastman, worked in the gift shop at the Green Valley for many years. I loved going to see her ... and having the Mickey Mouse sundae!

Jason: I worked there as a young man, washing pots. It was my first job. The kitchen staff was wonderful people. It was also my first time eating Salisbury steak. I felt so fancy — and the Mickey Mouse ice cream was the BEST!

Jeff: Had many family meals at the Green Valley as a kid (circa 1963-71). They mixed a mean Buck Rodgers (which was a boy's version of a Shirley Temple and a gateway drink to Old Fashioneds). Dessert of choice was Mickey Mouse ice cream. Do you think they got Disney's permission for that?

Dianne: What was this Mickey Mouse ice cream?

Jane: It was a rounded scoop of vanilla ice cream with two chocolate wafers for the ears, or so I recall, with a red maraschino cherry for the nose, chocolate chips for the eyes, and chocolate sauce as well. All kids – including me, my bro and my sis – went crazy for it!

Stacey: My grandmother loved this place and it was a special treat to take her there. She'd get all dolled up. She'd order a gimlet because it came shaken in a little carafe, which held two. She would have her cigarette holder, always bedazzling, and smoke her Kent cigarettes, which she bought on trips to Florida. She was the best, and this was her spot to really shine when she was older. I loved it too.

Marlene: "Swanky," as we used to call it!

David: The Green Valley was my mother's favourite restaurant back in the day, when we went out for special dinners. It was all done up with the white linen and fancy table settings. We were very young, but we were also taught that you had to behave at dinner. Whenever we drive past, it brings back memories of times gone by.

Diane: My dad used to take his mom there on Sundays after church. It was the highlight of the week for grandmother. The tree was beautiful, and so was the Green Valley Restaurant!

Donald: I took my mother there for wonderful suppers. Great food, and great atmosphere for families. Alas, nothing here remains for long.

(SHARED BY JOHN MYERS)

Streetcars in Ottawa

Streetcars are always a popular topic of discussion at Lost Ottawa. So when I came across several video clips in September 2015, I put them together into a short movie, than added some traffic noise and a little music.

What I didn't know was where the various scenes were shot, so I asked the community. It turned out they were mostly from the east end and Rockcliffe.

The trolleys seemed to whip along the streets in the original footage, but I decided not to edit the speed of the clips, which led to some discussion ...

Grant: These short clips are amazing. I'm too young to remember them, but my parents had lots of streetcar stories.

And: I remember the streetcars as a child. Lovely film.

CANADA SCIENCE AND TECHNOLOGY MUSEUM MAT-01008)

Anneke: The first clip is the Cobourg Street Barns, built in 1908. The second is Confederation Square, and the rest are all out towards Rockcliffe. Clip 3 with the kids cycling is Springfield, heading south. Clip 4 is Beechwood, heading east from Springfield toward Hemlock. Clip 5 is heading up from Beechwood into Rockcliffe Park, towards Maple Lane. Clip 6, not quite sure.

Paul: Awesome! Beechwood Avenue is just as I remember it as a small boy in the late-'50s.

Janet: My dad used to drive the Bank Street car. One day I was going uptown and he let me "drive" the streetcar! What a thrill. (Of course, I wasn't really "driving" it!) A memory that will never fade! How many kids have had that experience?

Kathy: I remember going downtown with my mom from the Bank Street terminal at Bank and Grove. Then going straight down Bank to Caplan's, where we would dress up and wear white gloves. Great memories!

Mary: My dad, Frank Harris, drove streetcars back in the '40s. I used to go with him to the booking, at the old barns on Albert St.

Kenneth: I'm quite surprised by the speed. I think of streetcars as moving much slower.

Derek: Did you speed up the frames per second, because the little Red Rockets are whipping through Ottawa's streets and dales faster than any TTC vehicle I've eve seen.

Barry: If our streetcars travelled that fast they would never have got rid of them — 8mm helps!

Mark: They could go quite fast if they had room to open up (like the Britannia Line).

Paul: Loved that trip out to Britannia (about 65 years ago.) My how things have changed.

Barry: The Britannia right of way from Richardson's Crossing was a blast. We used to sit in back and jump from one side of the car to the other, trying and make the trolley contact jump off.

Andy: Those were the wonder years! Or should I say these are the wonder years ... when we wonder what it would be like to be back there again!

Michael: This is terrific. Brings back lots of memories. I remember streetcars on Byron Ave. They should never have removed them.

Sylvain: Ding ding! There was something special about that mode of transportation. We should bring it back.

Patrick: Cool clip and too bad the streetcars are gone. I think I still have tokens somewhere to pay for the ride!

Chick Hatchery Again

(CANADA SCIENCE AND TECHNOLOGY MUSEUM J-19975-13)

Ah yes, the chick hatchery at the Science and Tech Museum on St. Laurent, shown here during Christmas holidays in '68.

The hatchery is always a popular post on Lost Ottawa, but this one was special because the hatchery's designer, Alan Todd, posted a comment, finally giving us the secret as to why it looked like a space ship, but really wasn't.

Alan: It is really touching to have so many people acknowledge the Science and Tech chicken hatchery. I designed it in the days of Claes Oldenburg. I had an interest in pop art and my concept for the hatchery was that of a fried egg — a humorous irony in my mind. Museum Director Dr. David Baird was not informed about my little joke until after the hatchery was built and put on display. In spite of my little deception about the form, Dr. Baird regularly celebrated its popularity. He was always interested in a good story.

Gerald: Great thing to see up close as a kid, because the eggs were usually in different stages of hatching. There would often be a lot of kids standing there watching.

Andrea: I once sat for about two hours to watch one hatch! Refused to leave until I finally saw it happen!

Julie: I remember my nose on this glass as a little kid in '68, when I thought the hatchery was there so kids could take a baby chick home! I cannot count the number of times I went home chick-less and disappointed.

Debbie: I don't mean to be rude, but what the heck does that one kid have on her head?

Tasha: The hat the girl is wearing? Wow, I had forgotten about that style. What were we thinking?

Annette: The fur hat with the pompoms? Love it, and used to have one very similar, back in the day.

Elizabeth: I guess she really wanted to fit in that day!

Linda: I had one of those mufflers. That furry thing you put around your neck and put your hands in to keep warm. Mine had a little change purse on top.

Annette: The hatchery was my favourite spot to visit, along with the crazy kitchen. Many fun hours spent there as a child.

Elaine: Crazy kitchen was the best!

Cynthia: Kids used to love it!

Marty: We lived a few blocks away from there. We knew it so well we could walk in the kitchen and look straight.

John: I lived about two blocks away in the '60s and early '70s. The museum was free back then, so we went to see the kitchen, chicks, trains and cars frequently. It was a favourite outing for me and my buds.

Bill: I spent hours in that museum at least once a month. Loved climbing the trains, too. Then off to roller skate at the Skadium!

Janice: I used to buy fertilized eggs for my kindergarten class to incubate from the farmer who supplied the museum. He would meet me in the parking lot of the museum before it opened and we would exchange money and eggs. Top-secret spy stuff!

Phil: I had a part-time job as a guide in the late '60s. We were instructed to reply to the question "where do the chicks go?" with a smile and say, "Oh we send them to a farm." Actually, they went to baby chick heaven.

Getting Ready for the Rink

A sign of the times — wintertime that is — is getting the Rideau Canal ready for the coming snow and cold. It is a tradition that's been going on 183 years. Some ancient rhythms are far from Lost.

Matthew: I was down there on Friday and there was a large crane removing one of the gates. You can see in this picture that the left gate is missing. Even historical items need repair.

John: Matthew, are you referring to yourself?

Mathhew: I suppose I could be considered an historical item. Unfortunately, well beyond repair.

Scott: And why do they drain it every year?

Gail: To become, once again, The World's Longest Skating Rink.

Jeannie: Also, so that the walls don't crack with the expanding ice.

Tyler: That's the real reason, to prevent damage to the walls of the canal.

Glenn: And protect the locks as well.

David: I'm sorry but I have to ask. I've been wondering since I was a kid. How do they drain the canal and where does all the water go?

Meaghan: According to an NCC FAQ, they drain it by opening the "sluice valves" on the Ottawa locks, near Parliament.

Aliza: The water flows from the canal system (opening the locks to let the water flow) into the river, then out to the St. Lawrence.

Tom: When I was living on Rosedale Avenue in Ottawa South (46 years ago) you could see the most amazing stuff in the canal after the water was drained! Old washing machines, car parts, and an incredible assortment of junk!

Mike: I remember reading somewhere that at some point in the '50s a city council of the day considered filling in the canal to lay rail tracks. I wonder if that is true?

Jennifer: The railway tracks already ran up the east side of the canal to the train station across from the Chateau Laurier.

Max: The decision in the '50s was actually to remove the tracks.

Glenn: There were, however, a number of earlier proposals to fill, or partially fill in the canal. The one I saw from the 1910s would have facilitated a subway along the north side of Wellington Street that then swung down to the west side of the canal. But I think the canal was at greatest risk during the '30s, after commercial boat traffic ended and before the canal became a tourist attraction. Even then, part of the canal was filled in between the University of Ottawa and Bank Street in order to build what is now Colonel By Drive. This did take place during the '30s. Before that, Echo Drive was the street that ran closest to the canal edge.

David: I can remember moving to Ottawa from Europe in '84. I had just settled into a routine, and didn't really know about draining the canal. Coming home from work one day, I alighted from the bus, and saw that – SOMEBODY HAD STOLEN MOONEY'S BAY! It was quite a shock!

(LOST OTTAWA)

The Lost Cinemas at Place de Ville

Looking around for an evening picture to post in November 2015, I came across a story on Ottawa Rewind about the abandoned movie cinema in the Podium Building of Place de Ville, and put up a photo of the cinema taken from Sparks Street.

I learned there were actually two theatres in the Podium, one stacked on the other for a combined seating of 1,200, connected by escalators.

Opened by Famous Players in '71, the theatres were closed in '96, but the space was never repurposed. Many people were surprised to learn that there was ever a theatre there. Some had ideas on how the space could be used again.

Anik: I have walked by the back doors many times and always wondered where they went.

Patricia: I remember going to shows there. I had no idea the space still existed.

Mike: I can't believe it is still there. They should open it up for tours.

Michael: I have worked across the street for the past 16 years and remember going to movies there.

Andrew: No way! I work at the Delta and an old cinema has been across the street the whole time? Crazy!

Karen: Got my first job there in '79 or '80, making and selling popcorn. Ran up and down those escalators many times! There was also a small lounge upstairs with pinball machines.

Jeannie: That was my favourite theatre to go to as a child. I loved going down the escalator.

Sean: I used to love this cinema. I saw my first movie without parental supervision there in '87. I was sad when it closed. Not as sad as when the Rideau Centre closed ... but still.

Laurie: Saw the movie Papillon with Steve McQueen at this theatre.

Tricia: I so remember this theatre, seeing Puff The Magic Dragon with Jenny and Auntie Mo.

Moyra: Saw Grease there in Grade 7!

Daniel: I saw the Care Bears Movie and Clue.

Stefanie: My dad used to be the manager at that theatre and I would go with him to work. I would run around the theatre before it opened for

the day. I also remember seeing a special midnight screening of Batman Returns. Good times!

Andre: I saw Batman (1989) at Place de Ville. I think Batman Forever and Cliffhanger were the last movies there.

Andrew: I saw the original Superman movie there.

Chanta: Bill and Ted's Excellent Adventure!

David: Sat through Blazing Saddles. Twice!

Dan: Saw Enter the Dragon there several times in '73.

Rosemarie: My husband and I had one of our first dates in this theatre. We went to see The Way We Were — and that was the last chick flick he watched with me!

Sara: It's so unfortunate that Ottawa cannot support mainstream movie theatres in the heart of the city.

Chris: Ottawa should have tried to take advantage of this venue for the European Union Film Festival. Lineups on Rideau Street at night, in a dodgy part of town, will not do the festival any favours.

Felix: It could be a great mid-sized concert venue in downtown Ottawa.

Vern: That cinema would make a great venue for a resident Children's Theatre Company! If it is just abandoned, the owners could donate the space to a non-profit company for a tax write off! And, since there are actually two theatres, one could be a rehearsal space for the next production! I'm in!

The Record Snow Again

It seems people in Ottawa can never get too many pictures of the record-setting winter of 1971-72. They certainly loved this picture of snow piled up to the roof of a suburban home in Alta Vista.

People shared all sorts of stories about that winter. I still have nightmares about the shoveling.

Michael: My outlandish claim that the snow was up to the eaves was always ignored. Well!?

Patricia: I remember we couldn't see out the front window. Just like this picture!

Alex: That was my first winter in Ottawa – incredible.

Rose: We moved into our new home the third week of October '71. By mid-December we had so much snow piled up in the front yard we could only see roofs across the street. The snowplows kept breaking down because they were still trying to push the snow onto the lawn.

Natalie: My sister and I climbed the snowdrift to the top of our roof and went sledding one morning – until the babysitter cottoned on and just about had a heart attack! We were five at the time.

Carolyn: We could step from the snowbank to the roof. Backyard fences had disappeared. The kid's swing set was buried to the top bar.

Susan: I remember my dad sending us down the driveway once, to check if we were at the right house. Also tobogganing on the roof!

Barbara: As kids we had a great time with all the sliding and fort building. We spent most of our free time outside back then.

Patricia: And amazingly enough, you lived to tell about it!

Keith: I remember I was 11, living in Nepean and having to toss the snow many feet above my head.

Joyce: We had just moved from overseas, where our biggest snowfall had been four inches. We had only one shovel and a 100-foot driveway!

Sharon: I loved that winter. Not so sure my dad or older brothers did!

Lynne: I remember we were trapped in our house. Our neighbour used his snowblower to clear a path to our front door.

Dave: I remember this winter very well. One weekend, 20 inches fell. The snow banks beside the driveway went up to the eaves of the house. I couldn't toss the new snow over the banks until I lopped off the tops of those damned things. Parents got a snowblower the NEXT year. After I had left home for university.

David: This was the winter I started up a fixed-price snowblowing business as a teenager. My hourly wage was pennies.

Ian: I remember putting a small flag on the top of my car's radio antenna so other people would see me over the snowbank as they pulled out of their driveways!

Louise: Got my driver's license that winter. Now I know how to drive in snow!

Patti: I went in the ditch.

Joy: My mom had to take the bus to work and when the driver opened the door for her to get out the snowbank was piled up to the hydro lines!

Richard: I remember driving on the Quebec side, near Quyon, and having to abandon our car and seek shelter at a farmer's house. Stayed two nights until the road reopened.

Sabina: I was born that winter and recall my mom telling stories about how, as they drove to the hospital, they could see people standing on top of bus shelters.

Susan: Tales to tell the grandkids now!

Nancy: The good old days.

Gloria: Remind me never to emigrate to Canada. If I should have a slip in memory, don't let me in.

(CANADA SCIENCE AND TECHNOLOGY MUSEUM, STOWELL COLLECTION)

Britannia Drive-In Re-Visited

September 18, 2015: 3,002 likes, 1,561 shares, 428 comments and 193,187 reached

(GeoOttawa)

Friday Night in Lost Ottawa. Time to jump in the trunk and sneak into the Britannia Drive-In?

With almost 200,000 views, more than 3,000 likes, and 428 comments, this post about the Britannia Drive-in was by far the most popular post on Lost Ottawa in 2015.

Helen: Twenty-foot long Country Squire Station Wagon? Check. Four squabbling siblings dressed in pajamas? Check. Playground with swings, but only during the dancing hot dog and popcorn intro? Check. Speaker ready? Check. Bring on True Grit!

Patricia: We would put the kids in their PJ's and the mattress in the back of the station wagon. Then it was off to the show.

Faye: I can remember mom, dad and all seven kids piled into our station wagon with lots of blankets and pillows. Big tubs of sandwiches, popcorn, and a water jug of Kool-Aid.

Marie: My mom would have a cooler for drinks and two huge bowls of popcorn. You could talk and ask questions, laugh and not be told to be quiet. It was a night that families could afford, not like now. We need to bring back the fun!

Phil: We used get the kids in their PJ's. They would bring their baseball mitts and play catch with a hundred other kids. Then, at dusk, the cartoon would come on and that was the cue for the kids to head back to their cars.

Jessica: I was one of those kids who played catch with the other kids before the movies! Would have been late '80s.

Bernie: When our first-born was less than a year old we made a little bed behind the back seat of our VW Bug (perfect for that) — and were denied admission to the drive-in because she was not 14!

Elizabeth: I remember when I was a little kid, going with my sister, brother-in-law, and their son. I went to the snack bar for the first time alone! When I got back to the car, I tried to get in. My nephew had jumped around his dad's neck and my sister had thrown herself over his lap, and when I stuck my face in the window to see what their problem was — that's when I realized I was trying to get into the wrong car!

Kathy: The drive-in was a cult. On a long weekend the cars would line up forever, you ate all kinds of junk, you could bring kids in their pajamas, they had swings sets, you could go with a bunch of girls ... but you were cautious about going with a guy!

Ron: If you had a station wagon like my Mom's '63 Fairlane you could load it up, park in the back row facing the wrong way, and put a couple of lawn chairs on the roof and tailgate. Great memories!

Jayne: I remember going there in my brother's little Austin Mini with six of my "closest" friends. We were 16 years old. Fun times. We'd follow up the movie with a skip across the road to the Tai Ping Chinese Restaurant.

Gary: I experienced a number of firsts at this drive-in when I owned a '54 Hudson Hornet! Nuff said!

Martin: Fond memories of making out in the back seat of my huge old Chevy.

Gail: I met my husband of 54 years at this drive- in. I remember the night very well!

Anita: You didn't tell us you met dad there!

Sean: My battery died there while watching a double header. It took CAA two hours to show up.

Shawn: Same here. Girlfriend was not impressed. Still married me.

Jane: That opening line is so accurate. I don't think I ever went inside the car. Always stuffed in the trunk!

Lee: Good times. Two people in the front, two in the back seat, two people and a case of beer in the trunk!

Daryl: It was a rite of passage to sneak in at least once.

Peter: I was an usher there in the early '50s and it was always funny to lean against a car that had smuggled people in, yelling at the driver to let them out.

Steve: Man, we used to turn the lights off in my VW golf and drive in through the exit! Halfway in, we would turn off the car and roll into the lot!

Barry: We took our bikes and sat in the back rows, behind the cars and beside a speaker. Occasionally they'd kicked us out, but if it they weren't busy they'd let us stay.

Tom: In the '70s we used to walk to the drive in and sneak under the fence. We called it a date.

Saundra: We would hop the fence, sit beside a car to listen, watch the show, and keep an eye out for the flashlights!

Peter: I remember climbing up on the fence and sitting there with my friends, watching movies with no sound!

Dawna: I lived on Bayshore Dr. and remember watching movies from the fence, thankful the cars by the fence had turned up their volume.

Gail: When I was a kid, my girlfriend's parents had a cottage down the road from the drive-in. We would walk in and they had lawn chairs at the front for people to sit and watch the movie.

Lorraine: I used to ride my bike to the drive-in and sit on benches at the front.

Paul: My grandmother used to have a house that backed into the theatre. In the summers I discovered I could tune into the movie audio with a radio.

John: I could see the movies playing from my apartment in the early '80s.

Janice: My grandma lived in the apartment building next door and her bedroom window faced the drive-in. When we were little, my sister and I would sneak over to the window and watch adult movies whenever we slept over. Next morning we would be woken up by the hundreds of seagulls that swarmed the parking lot, eating all the dropped popcorn.

Stacey: We lived just off to the west side of the screen and my grandparents lived behind the drive-in. To me, the sounds of summer include the honking horns as dusk set.

Heather: Honk, honk, honk! At the same time every night and seagulls every morning at five a.m. How could I forget? Thanks for the memory!

2016

Learning to Skate at Fisher Park

January 2, 2016: 229 likes, 21 shares, 54 comments and 14,319 reached

(SHARED BY HEATHER CRYSDALE)

Here's an iconic shot of something hundreds-of-thousands of people in Ottawa have done — learn to skate on an outdoor rink.

This one was shared by Heather Crysdale, who wrote:

"Who remembers skating at the outdoor rink at Fisher Park? This is where I learned to skate, and here is my brother and I in 1966."

Pierre: Recognized this as Fisher Park even before reading the caption. I was born in 1975, so it hasn't changed much! I worked down the street at Valiquette Sports (corner of Wellington and Huron). Sharpened many a skate there!

Arthur: I skated at Fisher Park before the war. At that time, there was a hockey rink in the middle with a general skating rink around the outside. It also had a heated change shack with a wood stove. You could leave your shoes and not have them stolen — and this was the Depression.

Diane: Skated there around '55. I remember the four posts in the centre of the rink, with big lights, and speakers playing Blue Danube. I remember the shack where we would go to warm up and even sit on top of the furnace to keep warm. I lived on Huron, so it wasn't too far to walk.

Jacquelin: Diane, your description brought tears to my eyes. It was just like that. The best outdoor rink. We lived on Hilson in Westboro and took the streetcar over, usually in the evening.

Vern: The Fisher Park rink was the one I remember because it was actually two rinks. The hockey rink with boards was surrounded by the skating rink, so there was never a conflict with those who wanted to play hockey and those who just wanted to skate. But my first memories of an outdoor rink are of Grant School in Britannia.

Peter: I used to skate at Fisher Park regularly in the early '60s. Friday and Saturday nights they had recorded music playing, and I can remember going round and round to the Skaters' Waltz.

Peter: As a kid growing up in the neighbourhood, in the '60s and early '70s, this was the place to be after school. No day was complete without a stop at Mike's (as it was called in my time) at the corner of Harmer and Kenora, which I see in the background there.

Margaret: Learned to skate on our backyard rink, but also on the outdoor rink (with changing rooms and cook shack) in Cumberland, Ontario. My dad used to play music for the public skating there — I remember it as if it were yesterday! Sad day when it was enclosed.

Barbara: I have super memories of skating and hockey playing at the outdoor rink in Britannia Park. The first year of the first Britannia girls' hockey team was played at that rink. We ran to the warm-up hut between shifts!

Louise: In the '80s, we skated on the river in Orleans. Well, more of a swamp, near the river.

Marilyn: Brewer Park. Little potbelly stove in the shacks. Put our snowy mitts on it to sizzle and dry.

Doug: We skated at the City View Public School rink in the early '60s, which was complete with lights, boards, and a change room. We lived on Canter Boulevard, so we would put our skates on at home and walk to the rink. Don't remember ever sharpening the skates, though!

Laura: The best was the year my dad made us a rink at the little house we lived in on Evered Ave. We spent all day outside, and snow was a good thing. Now we can't get out of the car fast enough to elude the white stuff.

Largest Midway on Earth

Bird's Eye View of the entrance to Ottawa's Central Canada Exhibition in the '50s, featuring a sign that says: "Largest Midway on Earth!"
This was the Ex in its prime.

Heather: My first memory of the Ex was climbing under the fence, then meeting Elsie the Cow all decked out with flowers. Huge thrill.

Jacquelin: I remember Elsie. I believed she was the real one on the Borden's milk carton.

Monica: Remember the invisible dogs on leashes that they would walk around selling? Anyone get one of those as a kid? I remember the first time I saw that as a child ... amazing!

Tom: When I was a kid we lived a block away at Fourth and O'Connor. Nobody cared much about the noise, and people in the neighborhood made good money renting space in their yards, laneways and lawns for parking. Plus, we could sneak in under the fence by the Driveway. Often, right into the area where the carnies had their trailers.

Charlene: We used to park cars for the whole week, and made enough money to pay for the last day of the Ex.

Tom: My dad worked at the Ex. After it closed for the day, the staff would gather at the Horticulture Building. Around 3:30 a.m. dad would start to lose it, so we would go and tour the Largest Midway on Earth. Just let me say, some of those carnival people ... well, they scarred me for life!

Cheryl: My father also spent time employed here, but I think he probably sneaked off with a "dance girl." Loved the Ex!

Marilyn: I especially loved it as a kid because my dad worked there every summer and we got to go on all the rides for free.

Vince: I have a lot of good memories of the Ex. The best are of food kiosks run by local churches who used real — not frozen — beef patties for their burgers. More than a few of us snuck in over the fence, the wafting aromas of burgers, fries and carny foods singing to us with their siren call.

Sue: Fresh burgers with fried onions and green peppers ... YUM !

Vince: One of the churches always had two-for-the-price-of-one burgers and hot dogs.

John: St. Giles Church was at the back end of the Coliseum. Greasiest and best food on the planet.

Vince: A couple of the United Churches were excellent and St. Hyacinth's Church, too.

Ruth: My best food memories are: Tiny Tom Donuts (made fresh as you watched), candy apples, cotton candy, and hot dogs from the Shriner's food stand at the front entrance to the Cattle Castle. Worked there for several summers as a teenager to make some extra spending money for the new school year. I looked forward to the Ex with mixed emotions. Loved the money, hated the thought that school would start the week after.

Sue: Growing up in old Ottawa east, we would walk along the canal everyday to attend the Ex. I was a ride fanatic but also enjoyed going through the buildings to check out all the exhibits and eat the food. When I was older I modeled at the "Where It's At" Building. Every visit ended with the purchase of a bag of Tiny Tom donuts to eat on the walk home. Loved it and miss it!

Marty: Ahhhhhh, the Tiny Tom Donuts, watching them float through a river of grease ... But, damn, they were good.

Sue: I have awesome memories of the Ex as a kid, especially the Pure Food Building. One visit inside and you came out full from eating all the "free samples!"

Lorna: So much to see. And so much to eat!

Soapbox Racing

Ladies and Gentlemen, start your engines ... if you have an engine!

That was our tagline for this picture from the Ottawa Citizen, of a soapbox derby in Aylmer, September 3, 1956.

That was back in the day (in the late '50s and early '60s), when the Aylmer Lions Club sponsored an annual Labor Day Derby, in which up to a hundred boys — and girls — participated.

The races were always fun, what with wild crashes, wheels, and the possibility of even whole back ends flying off!

(CITY OF OTTAWA ARCHIVES CA040300)

Nancy: Now this is the kind of thing we need to bring back. Give kids a great reason to go out and create and play.

Pierre: Try doing it today and you'd end up in court.

Yvonne: Too risky. Too many liability issues! Hell, they don't even let kids play tag in schoolyards!

Phil: It would never happen these days. There would be way too many safety procedures, people complaining, and organizers that would be afraid that if a kid got hurt, they would get sued.

Fraser: You are so right. Helmet, gloves, full leathers, and a waiver signed by the kid, his parents, grandparents, and the family dog!

Deb: Actually, there are still a few derbies out there — Smiths Falls and Manotick come to mind.

Ed: The Optimist club of Spencerville held one a couple of years ago. For the life of me, I can't figure out where there is a hill in Spencerville.

Aline: I remember this one in Aylmer very well. What a fun time it was! Fathers and sons and family used to help build the cars. Everyone was so anxious for the race to arrive.

Bonnie: I don't think they have soapbox derbies in Aylmer anymore. I could be wrong. But I lived in Aylmer back then, and remember some of these kids' faces.

Hélène: My husband was the kid who drove the "Super Duper No. 5," shown on the left.

Nick: I'm in car #4.

Louise: I was also in the race! I recognize Frank and Jimmy O'Donnell, Tommy O'Gorman, some Beaucaire boys, Mary Lacourse, and Digue Mondoux. My brother Paul says he remembers it like yesterday.

Donna: Where's Frank and Jimmy? They are my cousins.

Louise: Frankie is two rows behind #13B. He is wearing a dark jacket, standing next to Mary Lacourse. Jimmy has #18 on his white t-shirt.

Donna: I thought #18 was Jimmy! I remember him driving his car down Main Street with me holding on to the side window on a skateboard. Imagine if you did this today!

Ed: Terry Smith and I built an official soapbox derby car in Grade 8. I can remember the steering failing and going from one side of the street to the other and still winning the race. What fun!

Marc: In the early '70s we had a soapbox derby using the hill on Main Street in Gatineau — but only once! The kids scared the poop put of themselves halfway down, and most crashed into the hay bales at the bottom.

The Vets

Up in the morning and off to work, from your suburban Ottawa home at the corner of Anna and Tunis Avenues, May 1956.

The intersection is just off Fisher, south of Carling. A lot of tiny homes, or "Vets Homes" as they were once called. I'll take one!

Pete: My dad used to refer to this neighborhood as "the Veterans' Section."

Liz: "Vets Village!"

Ronald: "The Vets."

Laura: Good solid homes built for WWII vets, and many of the streets in the neighborhood have military ties: Marshall, Admiral, Anna, Crerar, Tunis, Viscount, Harrold, Veteran, Crown.

Debbie: War bride houses!

Lee: They were built for vets returning from overseas, many with new brides and children. I was one of those children and my mom was a British war bride.

Andrea: My husband grew up on Harrold Place and his mom came over from Scotland as a war bride.

Frances: Not a wartime base, but the same plans for these veterans' houses were used by Wartime Housing Limited, which morphed into Canada Mortgage and Housing.

Erica: Little "war fours." Good old Central Mortgage and Housing.

Ann: Small by today's standards, but still a place a man and his wife and children would proudly call home.

Gail: Tiny, simple and perfect!

Diane: I live in a similar house in Heron Park, on Richard Ave. Built in 1950. I like to think of it as "sustainable" rather than "tiny!"

Isabel: The Citizen ran a story about the vets' homes, with a man who talked about coming home after work and walking into the wrong house because everything looked exactly the same!

Karin: The same plans were used at every RCAF base in Canada, so despite moving every two years, to four different provinces, my mother never had to adjust the curtains or carpets.

Charlene: Being a base brat, these remind me of my childhood.

Isabel: My dad had an old army friend who lived in the Vets. We used to visit often. They had a daughter who, believe it or not, had been left on their doorstep!

Mike: Grew up at 225 Crerar in the '70s and '80s. Our neighbor was a vet who landed on D Day. He had great stories.

Jeff: I had my first paper route here, on this corner, for the Ottawa Journal. I also remember a bicycle shop was run out of a man's garage. He was a dealer for CCM.

Michael: We lived at 191 Anna, just near the corner of General, in the early '70s.

Gary: My friends lived at 192 Anna. We were the ones always working on our muscle cars.

Pete: Little Boxes! We grew up on Anna Ave. I went to Gowling for kindergarten! Remember it well. Great Trick-or-Treating on Halloween.

Christine: The houses were worth about $6,000 then. Today?

Diane: They are worth anywhere from $350,000 to $400,000, depending on condition and upgrades.

Eric: Take me back in time ... please!

Wendy: You can have one of these homes today. Most of them are still there. In fact, the neighborhood looks even better because the trees have matured.

Murielle: I'll take one of those cars to go with it, too.

(CITY OF OTTAWA ARCHIVES CA038365)

How Not to Park on Baseline Road

Baseline Road in August 1956, looking east from Fisher Ave towards the Prescott Highway (as Prince of Wales was once called.) The fields of the Experimental Farm are on the left.

The road had been reduced to a mud track by heavy rains, and almost looks like it was being rebuilt at the same time. Somehow, not one, but two cars managed to slip off the shoulder and turn over.

One of them must surely have been wondering how the other guy flipped. Just before he did the same.

Cheryl: I believe it was being reconstructed, because when we moved out to Carleton Heights in the fall of 1956, I remember Baseline Road as paved, and Fisher Avenue paved only as far as Baseline. Past Baseline, Fisher was a gravel road. I felt like we were moving to the end of the world.

Glenn: Shows what Baseline was like when it was a rural road, and it was still only a two-lane road when I was a kid. It would have been widened likely around 1966-67, when the Heron Road Bridge opened.

Cory: Grandmother always talks about how Baseline Road used to be a dirty farm road. Now I see what she meant.

Heather: I can't believe this is Baseline. OMG.

Jacki: No one would believe Baseline was once like this, until they saw this photo.There just needs to be a cow or two.

Mark: Hard to imagine folks living in the Capital of Canada volunteering to live in a suburb with this backwater dirt road as its main exit – or that this backwater dirt road is now Baseline Speedway.

Danny: Maybe it was the $14,000 houses and no other places to go?

Eric: Sign me up!

Michel: Most of those houses are still there.

Diane: Right near the Autosky Drive-In.

Cindy: I lived in one of those houses when I was a young child in the early '60s. One day in 1963 or '64, when I was two-or-three years of age, I decided to take a walk by myself down this stretch of Baseline. My mom didn't even realize I was gone until some nice man appeared at the door with me in tow. Typical. Thank you to that wonderful man!

Rob: Nearby was Dynes Farm, which wasn't sold until the late-'50s. It was deliciously rumoured that the family then moved to a mansion off the canal near Mooney's Bay. The Russ Fawcett Golf Driving Range ran along the eastern end, off the Prescott Highway near Hog's Back.

Nancy: Cars used to fall in the ditch there a lot.

Danny: Claude, is that you in the picture?

Claude: OMG, I remember that. I was cool back then!

John: I go by there every day. SAVE THE FARM!

Ottawa's Other Chateau

When people in Ottawa say "Chateau," they usually mean the Chateau Laurier. But there is, in fact, another Chateau — the Chateau Lafayette, next to the Irving Rivers clothing store in the Byward Market. Shown here in the mid-50s, the "Laff" (as it was often called) has recently been completely renovated, but once it was one of the city's most celebrated dives, with cheap beer served in little pilsner glasses or quarts, free beans, a great jukebox, a shuffleboard table and, let's just say an awful lot of character.

Dave: When I drank at the Laff the beer was 10 cents for a draft. The Grand Hotel was even better. Free beans or macaroni on Fridays. With a ten cent beer.

Jack: I worked for Zunder's Fruitland in 1969-70. I remember drinking underage at the Grand and the Lafayette, too.

Nick: The regulars in this picture were still there in the '70s. Now it's been renovated. I hope they kept the jukebox with Coltrane on it.

Wanda: The Laff had the best jukebox in town.

Johanne: My dad would drop in for a beer every Saturday when he went to the vegetable market.

Jean: Mr. and Mrs. Renaud had their vegetable kiosk out front for nearly 60 years.

Natalie: Remember when you could buy live chickens on the median in front of the store?

Tom: When I was a kid in the '50s, it was possible to buy not only live poultry, but also rabbits, and even lambs and kids (goats!).

Mark: Ottawa's other Chateau! While working for the Haunted Walk of Ottawa a few years ago, I used to take people to the Laff at the end of the Naughty Ottawa Pub Walk. It was great fun watching the reaction to the old "Ladies and Escorts" sign hanging up in the corner of the bar and of course their on-the-ceiling work of art.

Heather: Early to mid '70s, I remember the waiters (always men) had to legally (I think) "wear" a tie, so they would clip one end of the bow tie onto the open neck of their white shirt and let the other end dangle. "Quarter draft" (25 cents) and pickled eggs with a cellophane packet of soda crackers. Came in a small cardboard tray, maybe 25 cents also.

Nancy: And cigarettes were 35 cents a pack.

Tom: For years after I started hanging at the Laff, the only "drinks" available, were beer, and ... beer. Draught or bottles, pints (12 oz.) and quarts (22 oz.)!

Glenn: Hands up who hasn't had a quart in The Laff!

Paul: I seem to remember the Lafayette as one place you could still get beer in quart bottles many years after other bars stopped selling them.

Christopher: I remember drinking quart bottles there in the early '90s. A great mix of people.

Geoff: When I was in university in the '90s, they sold beer for $2.50. If you ordered two and handed them a five, they'd put them back in the fridge.

Susan: I paid 25 cents a glass and $2.00 for a pitcher.

Danny: Those little pilsner glasses you mention held seven ounces and were two for 35 cents in my day. I won't comment on when that day was.

Mark: I spent much of my time and tuition money down there at the Chateau Lafayette. So awesome. Wouldn't trade a moment!

(CITY OF OTTAWA ARCHIVES CA018507)

The World's Biggest Bomber Pays a Visit

An unusual visitor came to Ottawa on September 25, 1956. The world's biggest bomber, otherwise known as a B-36.

The plane, with it unusual combination of six pusher propellers and four jet engines, was here for a Cold War airshow at Uplands Airport, which was then a major airbase.

With a crew of 15, the B-36 was 162 feet long and 47 feet high. It had a wingspan of 230 feet, carried a payload of 84,000 pounds, and enough fuel to fly 10,000 miles without stopping, which was calculated to be enough for a (1950s) car to go around the world 16 times.

(CITY OF OTTAWA ARCHIVES CA040731)

Bill: I know almost nothing about planes, but aren't the propellers on the wrong side of the wings?

Bram: Those are the "pusher props."

Rick: Six Turning, Four Burning.

Steve: Fascinated me as a kid. I had a model.

Mark: My dad saw a formation of these, flying relatively low overhead in the '50s. He said it shook the ground.

David: You have to like the Victorian-through-'50s design ethic — "Build Big." I can't imagine a modern air show being quite as impressive, what with a drone the size of my Toyota, and a cruise missile the size of my bicycle.

Gary: First time I've seen a picture of this. I always thought the B-52 was the biggest back then.

Phil: This was on its way out by '56. The vastly superior B-52 was starting to enter service in '55.

Curtis: A couple Beech 18s; 4 T-33s; 3 CF-100 Canucks, and an early straight-fin Cessna 310 (I think) are also on the tarmac.

Mike: The Avro Arrow was under development at this time, and was about 1 1/2 years away from flying.

Teri: My father worked on the Arrow. I remember vividly the day he came home in tears. Feb 20, 1959.

Michael: A disgraceful Diefenbaker betrayal. Still makes me boil — though I was but a child when the treasonous deed was done. Killing the Arrow project to appease American aerospace industry.

David: Another plane that was also beautiful ... I got to sit in the Arrow cockpit when pieces were on display at the Ottawa airport flight museum [before it moved to the Aviation Museum in Rockcliffe — ed.].

Brian: One B-36 crashed in Labrador. I think another crashed on the west coast, maybe B.C.

Carson: Yes, it was BC and an atomic bomb was reported on board.

Scott: The B-36 was notorious for catching on fire, due to the poor cooling of the engines.

Geoff: Its 4-row, 28-cylinder radial engine had a bad habit of lighting on fire and if you didn't start the engine properly, it fouled all 56 of its spark plugs!

David K: I had a Chrysler K-car like that!

David E: It was known as the Convair Peacemaker.

Paulmatt: The tragedy being that no drink has been named after it.

Critical Care at
the General Hospital

You need signs to find practically anything in a hospital, but I had to laugh when I saw this one at a junction in the hallways of the General Hospital on Smyth Road.

There's something quite Canadian about a sign to Tim Horton's in Critical Care.

Joyce: Too funny.

Bob: As it should be!

Charlene: Timmy's is Canada, that's for sure.

Roma: Timmy's does cures me!

Cathy: Been there, seen that too many times!

Darlene: Coffee is essential for the eight-hour wait to be seen in emergency.

Bill: Tim's coffee is that bad?

Annie: But the arrow is pointing up, better times ahead!

Donald: I wonder what the criteria would be, to end up in this ward? Over eight cups of Tim Horton's a day? You suddenly find yourself driving from the cottage, 50 miles away, just to get to a Tim Horton's. I know I have a problem ... but I'm not ready for this place yet!

Laurence: As someone who volunteers at the Ottawa Hospital, I've had an equal number of inquiries about where some ward might be, and where the Tim Horton's is. They put the sign there to make is easier for people to find, as an alternative to the cafeteria.

James: What I find amazing is that every time I visit the hospital on business, there is an incredibly long lineup at Tim Horton's and much smaller lineups at the other coffee shops there. And most of the people waiting in line are staff, spending their entire break waiting in line.

Karine: That's so funny, but so true!

Starr: My sister has been getting chemo three times a month for the past six months. She says the hospital has the best Timmy's around.

Ruthanne: My husband says so, too! But they really make you work for the Timmy's at the General. It's all the way across the building.

Anneke: Thank God for Timmy's at the hospitals! I can't tell you how many times I have had to take my mom to the hospital and the only place to get a coffee and a snack that doesn't cost an arm and a leg, and isn't out of a machine, is at Timmy's.

Christopher: Yes, without Timmy's in the hospitals, how can we wait for things like health care and other stuff that hospitals do?

Blair: My mom was in intensive care for 61 days, and families can be there as long as 23 hours a day. We were there almost every day and really appreciated that Tim Horton's. Many times over!

(LOST OTTAWA)

Sarah: Tim's pays big dollars to use hospital space and to advertise. Given health care cuts by the government, I have no problems with hospitals trying to recoup cash via Tim's.

Ann: Timmy's makes you feel better just seeing the sign when you are at the hospital.

Aliza: Ottawa Civic has Second Cup as well as a Tim's on their "main street." They used to have a Baskin Robbins — where the flower shop is now. I was a candy striper there in the summer of '85 and worked in the ice cream parlour. Made a tuna fish sandwich for Dr. Keon once! That was a year or so after the Jarvik 7 implant made him famous. I knew who he was, and was a very excited 12-year old!

Miriam: I have news for you, in every hospital in Israel you not only have a coffee shop, you have a whole shopping centre.

Max: Tim Horton's at critical care must be the place where they have the coffee IV ...

Before the Sparks Street Mall

Saturday Shopping on Sparks Street, back in 1899. Dodge a few Ottawa Electric Railway streetcars, dodge a few buggies, and go about your business.

What actually surprises me about these early pictures is the number of bicycles, not to mention the rather formal attire of the cyclists.

Bicycles were so popular that the Gendron Bicycles store was right downtown at the corner of Sparks and Elgin, under the awnings, lower right. Gendron was one of several companies that merged to form CCM the following year.

Ted: Electric wires, telegraph wires, streetcars, fire hydrants and water mains – citizens who remember Bytown must have felt they were living at the cutting edge of miraculous progress and innovation and that the Age of Industry and Empire was reaching its zenith!

Glen: The invention of chain mechanism and pneumatic tires in the 1880s made cycling easy and comfortable. The 1890s saw a worldwide bicycle craze.

David: Bicycles were HUGE in the days before cars became affordable. It was freedom to travel for many, especially women.

Patricia: They would have been using bicycles to get to work. They were exciting novelties and affordable for working and middle class people, including working women.

Thomas: When I came to Canada in '57, I bought a bike for $5.00 and rode it to work every day, four-and-a-half miles each way. Sold it at the end of the summer for $7.00. Then bought a '54 Mercury Niagara.

Janet: My grandfather rode a bike to work in Ottawa. He never had a car.

Guy: These photos make you want to go back to those days and experience life back then!

George: Back when mommy and daddy didn't have to drive their wonderful little darlings everywhere they wanted to go! So they used bicycles and legs!

Rick: Back when people dressed in jacket and tie, or ladies in dresses, and hats were mandatory. Working folks put on overalls, but mostly had a tie on underneath. It was a different era. No one wore their PJs outside, or their trousers at half-mast!

Donna: I was on a bus on the Gatineau side and the traffic stopped. We looked out the window and there it was, bigger than life, making a pass over the Ottawa River. It was so low we could see the pilots. Glad I caught this bit of history.

Chris: I remember how low it was. The lawlessness of the '80s!

Debbie: I was working on Sparks Street at the time and it was amazing to see it flying overhead.

Allan: We watched it at Stats Canada from the R.H. Coats Building in Tunney's Pasture. Memorable sight.

Dwight: I was on a bus on Carling Ave. When we saw the shuttle the driver stopped, so we could all get out and have a look.

Neville: I remember coming home from work down Fisher Ave. as it flew over the Experimental Farm.

Dave: I was playing ball when it flew by Fisher and Baseline.

Susan: Flew right over us in Bells Corners. Felt like we could touch it.

Patricia: We lived in Borden Farm at the time. I stood on our picnic table and turned in a circle as a slow moving, white, 747 circled the city, piggy-backing the space shuttle! By the end of the circling I was having trouble seeing.

Graydon: I remember it flying over the house, then my mom took us to see it. I also remember the crazy traffic jam along the airport parkway.

Tanya: I remember my mother pulling us out of school to go see this.

Jason: My grade school class went to Uplands to see it. At ten years old, it was huge, and awe-inspiring.

Andre: I remember going to see this when I was three-years old. It started a lifelong fascination with space.

Jamie: I was there for all of it, at eight-years old, while my dad listened to his scanner waiting for it to fly over. Because of this event I was hooked on NASA's progress.

Christine: It was a big part of what inspired me to take a job with the Canadian Space Agency — even when it moved to St. Hubert, QC. Still thrills me all these years later.

VR: I had to marvel at American ingenuity when I saw it.

Michael: And here we are today with zero space shuttles. Yet there are iPhones everywhere.

Terry: Wait, let me get this straight. A plane can carry a space shuttle on its roof, yet the airlines charge us to check our baggage?

Elmdale Theatre 1962

Saturday matinee, perhaps, at Ottawa's Elmdale Theatre on Wellington, just past Parkdale. Date is probably 1962, unless that movie is a re-run. "Only Two Can Play" was a comedy starring Peter Sellers that came out that year.

The building is still there and is now as a church, but people remember the movies they saw there.

Cheryl: Spent many a Saturday at the Elmdale. Malted milk bars and a Coke. Lived just around the corner.

Anne: We were born and raised around there and used to buy a large popcorn for 10 cents. Certainly takes you way back!

Don: My brother Bill and I went every Saturday in the '50s. Tickets were twelve cents each.

Claire: We would go there regularly in the late '50s to watch movies, and sometimes on Saturday mornings they'd have yo-yo and bolo bat competitions.

Patty: Every Saturday the kids on the street would go to the Elmdale for a Western movie and cartoons. Magic!

Norm: During an intermission in the '50s, as a complete surprise (to me anyway!) Sach and Louis gave a live stage performance. That was a nice treat, because I loved their movies. Those were the days of 15 cents during the week and 25 cents on Saturdays. And you got to see two movies, a cartoon, and the news. Gee, I must be old!

Bruce: I spent many a Saturday afternoon at the Elmdale back in the 1940s and '50s, as well as at the Century and Nola. I saw the Bowery Boys there in person. Slip, Sach and Whitey were my favorites.

Christine: My Mom would send me to the movies on a Saturday when I was a kid. We lived just down the street off Parkdale. She would give me a quarter. Enough to get in and buy popcorn and a Coke.

Christine: I remember seeing Pillow Talk with Doris Day and Rock Hudson (watched it twice), McHale's Navy, Jerry Lewis movies, Charade, with Audrey Hepburn and Cary Grant, and many more.

Pearl: One of the first I saw was Elvis in Jailhouse Rock. That takes me way back!

Sylvia: This was the first theater I went to as a child. The movie was Sound of Music!

Jane: First movie I ever saw was Bambi! We grew up on Ross Street and referred to the area as the "West End." Theatres used to play "God Save the Queen" and "O Canada" at every showing.

Patty: We used to live on Grange. I loved seeing the Queen at the trooping of the colours at the end of the movie.

Fiorella: Those were the days ... when the ushers dressed nice and helped you find a seat.

Terry: My first movie on my own was Star Wars, at this theatre in 1977.

Scott: I remember seeing Star Wars and Fast Times at Ridgemont High there for the first time.

Hugh: Saw my first movie there – The Empire Strikes Back.

Fred: I remember lining up on a cold winter's night back in 1979, waiting to see Kramer vs. Kramer.

Coreen: I saw The Gods Must Be Crazy. It ran for over a year.

Peter: Last flick I saw there was Peter Pan with my nephew around 1992. Great theatre.

Sean: Last film I saw there was Howard the Duck. It was awful!

Cathie: Do you remember the woman who paced up and down the aisle making sure no one put their feet on the back of the seat in front? She was a bit scary.

Marianne: I was hoping someone would mention that matron who did not like feet on seats.

The Storyland Bunny

One of the fairytale characters from Storyland, spotted in a car lot along Highway 7 from Ottawa, just before the turn for Carleton Place.

Storyland was a theme park located near Renfrew that featured scenes from various children's stories. Opened in 1966, it closed in 2011.

The White Rabbit is now far from home!

Rhonda: Hello, Storyland Bunny! So glad you found a new home. You brought so much joy over the years to so many children.

Dwight: Now it's in Carleton Place selling cars!

Anneke: No wonder it looks startled.

Beth: Perhaps he hitched a ride because he was late!

Claudette: Missed the rabbit hole. Alice cannot be far behind! Sorry, couldn't resist ... I remember this dude and my kids still remember it, too.

Steve: Nice to see he still has his head. I remember back in the day people used to steal it.

Lexy: I drive past this on my way to the cottage. It's funny because they put a Mitsubishi symbol (I think) on the book he's reading, and I always laugh that he has that surprised look on his face while reading the car owner's manual.

Mike: I drove past this the other day. Recognized the strange bunny as soon as I saw it. Glad it found a home.

Emma: Had a cottage in Shawville. Came summer, when we were young, we always visited Storyland.

Sheri: We had a cottage near Pembroke and always stopped at Storyland at least once a season. Nice lookout there.

Cheryl: We used to pass Storyland back in the day, while driving to Portage du Fort to visit my grandparents.

Monique: We went there a lot as kids, and I brought my own kids there. I do remember hearing it was sold, but wasn't sure what they did with all the big characters.

Fiona: When they closed, there was an auction for all these big characters, I believe. I remember seeing the ad and thinking, "Gee, I want one!" Then I thought, "Where in God's name would I put it?"

Patricia: There is actually one rabbit still at Storyland, which has been converted into some sort of retreat/getaway. Can't remember the name of it.

Patti: It's called Elements.

Robyn: I didn't like Storyland. Thought the characters were creepy.

Nikki: You should have seen the clean up after it closed ... could have been a movie set for a horror film.

Barbara: There were two rabbits, I recall.

Nikki: Yup, two bunnies. The book one is much older than the fat one. Both sold for $3,000 at auction in 2013.

Coreen: I picked up Baby Bear, Cat and the Fiddle, the Big Bad Wolf and Red Riding Hood at the auction. It was awesome. I think Humpty Dumpty on the Wall also went for $3,000?

Nikki: Humpty went for $4,000 at auction and lives somewhere in Constance Bay now.

Celeste: That's amazing. I've been wondering where they all went.

Murray: There are more characters at Jak's in Portage du Fort, Quebec.

Jennifer: The shoe is at a house in Horton, near the highway.

Stephanie: One is still being loved by kids in Vars.

David: Fred Flintstone moons the cyclists on the Prescott-Rockland bike path, east of Orleans.

Shawn: Still have the crooked house?

Nikki: Snow White's cottage is still there, as are all the roads. Other buildings are still there, but have a different paint job on them. We kept a few more things at Elements ... like the two person outhouse by the beach!

(LOST OTTAWA)

The General Store in Britannia

The Britannia General Store in the early '60s. Playing no favorites, the store has signs for practically everything a beach-goer in Ottawa could possibly want to drink.

A little hard to see, but there's also a sign for Silverwood's ice cream, which made me think of ice cream bars.

In the original post, however, I made a typo and wrote "ice bream bars" ... which led to a question about Canadian character.

Tami: "Ice bream" bars? Is that fish-flavoured ice cream? You Canadians are weird!

George: If that's the store at the corner of Pinecrest and Carling, he was also the post master and local credit carrier. I heard he still had about $500,000 in credit owing when he died. I went in there many times.

Karen: This one would be at Howe and Britannia Road. It's an antiques hoarder store, where vendors rent space and sell their antiques. There have been renovations over the years, but I remember going in there when I was a young kid, buying candy.

Mike: I think that was Ayoub's. This is across the tracks on the west side of Britannia Rd. It would be torn down and replaced by Smiley's.

Gary: If I remember correctly, it was on the corner of Howe and Britannia road, at the streetcar right of way.

Debbie: It is still there.

Beverly: The store is still there, it's at the corner of Britannia Road at Howe Street, close to Britannia Park. I think they still sell beach stuff. There is an antique store on the opposite side as well as an ice cream shop, newly opened in what was previously a second-hand store.

Marjorie: Walked into this store a gazillion times as a teenager.

David: I'd go there now!

Bev: My sister Betty went to this store every day.

Janet: I might've been in there when they took this pic. I'm that old!

Jose: I Remember it well, and used to go there every day to get popsicles. What a great place to be a kid. So many great memories.

Ellen: Always a refreshing cold bottle of Pure Spring ginger ale and a bag of chips!

Ian: And Pure Spring soft drinks were bottled locally.

Ellen: We drank it all the time when we lived there. Even after moving to Niagara Falls, we never went without it, due to visitors/family, etc.

Guy: Always loved the distinct aroma of these stores ... a bag of chips and a Coke.

Charlene: How about Mello Rolls from Silverwood's dairy?

Sandra: I remember getting Mello Rolls at Joe's Confectionary in Westboro Village in the early '50s. They were five cents. One cent less than an ice cream, so a better buy!

Jack: How about the "double-dip" ice cream cones?

Shereen: Mom had a charge account at the store in the picture in the early '70s. Just the ticket for a couple of latch-key kids. If we could be called that, since no one locked doors! The Village was a wonderful place to grow up ... total freedom and safety ... great memories.

Ron: Britannia always had the best parties and some of the prettiest girls. Great dances at Lakeside Gardens too.

Peter: I loved Britannia Beach! When we hung out there, there were a lot of cottages and small summer homes. And corner stores. And the cutest girls in Ottawa.

Carol: Thanks!

The Clark Dairy Man Delivers

Breakfast in Lost Ottawa, with some fresh milk delivered by the Clark dairy man,in August 1959. Is that Mrs. Cleaver?

I noticed there are a lot of promos for buttermilk in these old dairy pictures — like the one on the side of this truck.

Then it was good for us. Now it's bad, some people say.

Lou: I remember the trucks, but I also remember the milkman delivering milk with a wagon pulled by a horse. Getting old, I think.

Janet: I remember the milkman leaving bottles outside our door. Also the bread man. And the rag man. Now, that really dates me!

Jamie: I lived in Carleton Place in 1957-58. Our milk was delivered by horse-drawn milk carriage. I would meet the milkman down the block and he would let me ride in the rig till I got to my house. I remember once, when the horse decided to take a walk while he was out of the vehicle ... with me in it.

Peter: I remember our milk arriving from Clark's in a horse-drawn wagon. There were big blocks of ice inside and on hot days the milkman might put the feedbag on the horse for a few minutes and chip off chunks of ice for the kids to suck on.

Rick: I remember Clark Dairy deliveries with horse and buggy. Our milkman really hated the change to trucks.

Marty: In the '50s, I used to help a man in the west end named John Burke. When he went from horse-and-wagon to truck, it took him longer to do his route. This was mainly because he had to go back to the truck after every customer. With the horse you could take enough milk to serve several customers in a row, and the horse would be waiting for you when you went back out to the street.

Liz: Our milkman was named Ed. He was so awesome. My mom left the money for him in the fridge. He called it "cold cash." Every so often he would leave us a carton of chocolate milk — his treat. Happy memories.

Michael: Our milkman from Clark's had big leathery hands and a big change purse on his belt, filled with "silver," which is what they called coins back in the day. A card in the window indicated whether or not you wanted milk that day. We lived on Switzer Avenue in Ottawa.

John: Every once in a while the Clark milkman would let me ride with him on deliveries. Just a few doors up mind you. But it was exciting for a little guy.

Barbara: My mom had the milkman and the bread man deliver to the house. It was great, and you got to know these people.

Lorie: I remember showing our milkman that I knew how to tie my shoes. That would have been around 1964 or '65 on McLeod Street. He was very encouraging.

Marilyn: Our milkman gave me a black cocker spaniel. Will always cherish those memories!

Sophie: I remember the milkman coming in and "fixing" our TV. When dad was at work. Hmmmmm.

Yvonne: What's this about the buttermilk? Who says buttermilk is bad? Next, someone will say condensed milk or cream is bad! Come on!

Pat: Buttermilk is not bad for us. It has more nutrients and calcium than regular milk. The only bad thing is the sodium ... so use in moderation, as in anything else.

Robin: If you can keep it down....

Andre: Tastes like goo, but makes a wonderful biscuit.

Brenda: The buttermilk used to taste like buttermilk. Now, I'm not sure what it tastes like. But I still drink it.

Vincent: You all see the buttermilk. I see ... "Hello, Mrs. Robinson."

The Carleton Tavern

(LOST OTTAWA)

This was one of our top posts for 2016. Perhaps no surprise. Established in 1935, the Carleton Tavern on Armstrong, behind the Parkdale Market, is one of Ottawa's most beloved taverns, and this is a city that loves its taverns.

The Carleton still has the two doors on front, an architectural memory of the days when there was one entrance for "Men," and another for "Ladies and Escorts." They still had that in '73 or so, when I first went there to enjoy the 35-cent beer.

Though long in the tooth, the Carleton is still going strong today.

Matt: My grandfather's watering hole.

Mallard: Great grandpa and grandpa Kennedy drank many a quart here.

Sammy: My grandpa and my dad both used to go there for pints and food, and when I moved to Tunney's, I started going there for breakfast. The guys there are great, and the staff is always really friendly and accommodating. Just a lovely place all around.

Leacy: This was where my dad would retreat to watch a hockey game when the five women in the house claimed the one TV.

Jocelyne: My dad's second home! He had his own stool at the bar and was such a regular the Saikelay family sent a huge flower arrangement to his funeral. Mom still lives around the corner, so I often go by the tavern. One day I should go in for a quart! Fond memories of the area.

Arthur: I remember looking for my father, who was the plumber for the Carleton, Elmdale and the Stirling. I always found him at a tavern.

Richard: Many a father-to-be waited there while his wife was busy at the Grace Hospital.

Aliza: When we go to the Parkdale Market, hubby always chuckles over the sign in the tavern window about their "babysitting" service.

Donald: The Carleton was a major Friday lunchtime place for those of us who worked for the feds at Tunney's pasture. Ordered pizza from the pizza place next door and would wolf it down with a few brewskys. Friday afternoons were not the most productive back at work.

Leona: I worked at Tunney's from '68 to '79. At Health and Welfare, as it was called then. I spent MANY a lunchtime at the Carleton, especially on payday when we got an extra hour or so to cash our cheques. I remember my first time seeing it, at the not-so-tender age of 21, and marveling at the stained glass windows and wood paneling. That same stained glass and paneling are there today ...

Neil: It was the watering hole of choice for many of the animators working on the Raccoons in the mid-'80s at the nearby Hinton Studio.

Christine: The Carleton was an old school hang out for us from Champlain High School in the '70s. I spent my last day of high school there.

Joe: Great drinking Mecca for Fisher Park boys back in the day.

Christine: I grew up around the corner from here, on Oxford Street. My grandmother would give me money to go down and buy Coke in a bottle for 10 cents and Humpty Dumpty chips in a cellophane bag for five cents. That was at the Carleton restaurant, attached to the tavern. I went to school with the owner's daughter. We attended Connaught and Devonshire schools. Great memories.

Sandra: I've worked at a few bars and I had the pleasure of working at this one. Definitely my favorite! Simon was a great boss. I worked with awesome staff and served a lot of great people! I have seen many different classes of people walk through those doors! When I wasn't working (and even when I was), it was my favorite place to be on Friday and Saturday nights. Always had great live bands and all-round terrific folks!

Children at the
Window of Murphy Gamble's

Children check out the Christmas display at Murphy Gamble on Sparks Street in December 1959. Above the children is a reflection of the Centre Theatre marquee beside the store, and the E.R. Fisher clothing store across the street.

Located at 118 Sparks Street, near Metcalfe, Murphy Gamble was one of Ottawa's favorite department stores. It was taken over by Simpsons in 1971, which closed its doors in '83. Now it's a Scotiabank building.

We posted a video of the inside of the store at the same time. Together, it made a great Lost Ottawa Christmas present!

(CITY OF OTTAWA ARCHVES CA024699)

Christine: Flashback to my childhood. The windows were mesmerizing.

Cathy: One of my favourite memories of Christmas when I was young.

Gail: The pic of the little girl could have been me. I was just over three and had a coat and hat just like her!

Tasha: It was scenes like this that helped create the magic of Christmas for us little ones.

Natalie: A "Norman Rockwell" moment.

Stephen: Murphy Gamble had excellent windows. Freiman's had spectacular windows. Remember the train on the fourth floor Toyland?

Lee: Oh, how well I remember the Freiman's windows and the displays inside. My aunt Ivy worked there for many years as a buyer for the ladies clothing department. Every year, I would visit my aunt, get an inside tour, and see Santa.

Debby: Freiman's did have wonderful Christmas displays, and the best malted milks!

Joan: Their malted milk was the best. I used to go over every day at lunchtime from work at the Daly Annex to have one. That was 55 years ago. Yikes!

Mary: Yum ... small glass for five cents. Don't forget the messages that flew by in their little cage!

Kathie: My auntie Bo worked in the restaurant area at Murphy's just up those beautiful stairs on the main floor. It had those round bar stools along the counter.

Marilyn: My grandmother loved to eat dessert on the mezzanine at Murphy's. Great store!

Adelle: Their sandwiches were to die for!

Brian: We would go to Murphy Gamble when my parents shopped downtown. I seem to recall an elevator with a cage and an operator.

Marlene: That brings back lovely memories of my years there, working in ladies' hats. The elevator operator wore white gloves and called out the floor.

Beverley: I remember the elevators. After watching the pretty elevator girls, I decided that's what I would be when I grew up.

Ann: My memory of this awesome store was being separated from my mother when I was around five. When the kindly clerk matron enquired if anything was wrong, I told her my mother was the one who was lost!

Margy: I miss that place. Lunch upstairs for a young secretary working on the Mall at AECB, showcases, purchases elegantly wrapped, nylons in boxes with tissue paper, very attentive sales ladies ... bring it all back please!

Pig Sled in the Byward Market

In Lost Ottawa you don't need a refrigerator when you buy ham in the Byward Market — but you do need your special pig-hauling sleigh!

Shown here in December 1926 and posted on New Year's Eve, 2016. Am I wrong, or is that kid smoking a cigarette?

Mike: Is that my Dad smoking there? He grew up on Guiges Street during the 1910s and '20s, and started smoking at age eight or nine. If it is, those two must've stolen that pig because they were starving in those days and had to steal food just to survive. Sad and funny, all at the same time.

Judy: Could be my dad, too. He grew up on George Street in the '20s, the youngest of five and quite the scallywag.

Giselle: My dad was born in '31 and started smoking at ten.

Randy: My grandfather told me once that he smoked cigarettes at ten years old, back in the '30s, to help him keep warm when he had to go out and chop firewood.

Pat: My parents started smoking when they were between eight and ten!

Susan: The good old days?

Bonar: In '26 cigarettes were still considered "a healthy source of energy and relaxation!" Don't you remember? And Coca Cola was still full of pure cocaine. "Gripe water" for babies was a solution of morphine.

Steve: And alcohol was prohibited. Cannabis had just been outlawed.

Aliza: Coca-Cola removed the "impurities" in 1905, so no more cocaine there.

Paul: Many kids smoked in those days. They hadn't yet been subjected to sensitive noses, government and whiner social engineering.

Ken: Yeah, but the poor guy probably died of lung cancer or emphysema, like too many others.

Renate: Guess you worked like a man and smoked like a man in those days.

Gaelan: Hey, if you were pulling a dead hog on a sled, you would want a cigarette, too.

Pauline: It takes a picture like this to remind us how far away from the small realities of life we, in this country, have wandered. Now very few people, especially children, get to see just where and how their daily food is acquired and processed.

Lynne: While it captures memories for so many, it was a hard life, certainly by today's standards. I'm thinking I could probably survive about a week — or less.

Sandy: Makes me appreciate Farm Boy!

Mike: Makes me think of smoked ham.

Paul: Mmmmmm ... bacon on the hoof.

Kevin: He'd walk a mile for a Camel ... and a Pig?

Grant: "Well you said you wanted a piggyback"!

Dave: If you are going to buy pork, it is better to go whole-hog!

Dan: You guys have revived one of my fondest memories. I was eight or nine years old, and had accompanied the men on "thrashing day,"

helping out as best I could. As we gathered in the milk house at the end of the day, one of the men said to my dad: "Here, he worked like a man, so let him have a taste of beer like a man." A half century later, it's still my most memorable sip of beer.

Margaret: This picture made me laugh so hard. So many of today's rules broken, so much that should be frowned upon. I do not know how we survived. That is one dead pig.

Chilly: They are so tricky to get in the oven otherwise.

Karen: Haul a pig? I can't get my boys to haul their posteriors out of bed.

Inside Bayshore Shopping Centre

September 27, 2016: 2,002 likes, 645 shares, 248 comments and 131,019 reached

This photo shows Bayshore Shopping Centre in the '80s, when the statues and the fountains were still there.

Shared by Coral Lynne B, the picture was viewed by an astonishing 131,019 people, our most popular pic of 2016.

Denise: "Lost Ottawa" in the '80s? Now I'm really feeling old!

Tony: Holy moly, I feel old, too. I worked there between 1981-84!

Frank: I'm so old I was at the grand opening of the Bayshore Mall.

EJ: I remember when Bayshore was a tiny strip mall with an ice cream place ... not that I'm old or anything.

Shawn: Not old. We just have great memories!

Coral: Pretty sure it was my grandmother who took this photo. It makes me miss the time when malls had water fountains! I definitely remember being so amazed by this as a little kid.

Ted: I loved those fountains, and was also amazed by them.

Lisa: Me too. It's the only thing I remember about Bayshore. I was ten-years old.

Jill: WHOAH! That statue was awesome, but also super creepy to me as a kid.

Constance: Looked like an alien invasion.

Jessica: I loved the beauty of the sculptures. To me they represented a celebration of life.

Paolo: "Celebrating life," that's a good way of putting it. It never failed to give me a smile, and take a few pennies of mine away.

Sokha: I used to ask my parents for their change, to throw in.

Matthew: I jump naked into the fountain when I was two and made a big scene, much to my mom's chagrin. I was looking for all the pennies.

Mitch: I concealed a magnet in the end of my floor hockey stick and used it to fish coins out of the fountain. My first job!

Joan: I started working at the Bay when the shopping center opened.

Patti: I worked there as a teen — at a jean store.

Jessica: Was the store called Jean Junction? My mom mentioned it was there in the 70s.

Dan: I was the manager of Warren's House of Britches.

Johanne: Who remembers Orientique? They sold incense ...

Jeff: I worked at Kinney Shoes and French Shoes ... a long time ago.

Jennifer: I worked at W.H. Smith Books in 1989.

Brenda: I worked at Pennington's in Bayshore from 1980-85.

Brigitte: I worked in the now defunct "Toyworld," from 1981-83.

Linda: I worked at the Little Farm Pet Shop and, oh, the stories! One time Blue, our macaw, flew right out of the store and landed on someone's back, then came back up the escalator. Now that was funny!

Janice: My high school sweetheart worked at Colour Your World, and spent most of his time admiring the pretty girl who worked in the store right across the mall.

Brenda: I worked one summer at the Bay Portrait Studio around '87, and then very briefly at the Parker Clean around '90. I was addicted to the peach juice from the Pik Nik.

Heather: My first job was at the second floor Pik Nik when Bayshore opened. I remember how loud the fountain was. I spent hours there.

Robert: Wasted countless hours in Bayshore as a kid. Either working at Pop84, the Bay, or chillin' at Pic Nik eating fries from a paper boat.

Ann: I worked at Miracle Mart for 4 years (1976-80). I remember ice cream cones from Laura Secord's and pogo sticks from Pic Nik at break time!

Jessica: When my mom was a teenager in the '70s, she worked as a cashier at Steinberg's. This was before there were barcodes and scanners. She had to manually punch in every price.

Andrea: Steinberg's! Man, you just brought back a flood of childhood memories.

Ann: Pinky Stamps!

Jessica: My mom said she spent a lot of her paycheques at Sam the Record Man.

Josée: I worked at Sam the Record Man. I remember sitting in those benches you see in the picture, smoking during my break. Seems so strange that we used to smoke inside.

Jesse: When T-Rex roamed the Earth.

Andrew: The mall only had two floors when this picture was taken?

Scott: Indeed it did.

Jessica: I always thought they had three. When was the third floor added?

Scott: The mall opened in '73 with two floors. The third floor was added in '87.

Eric: When the parking lot wasn't the hellish mess that it is now!

Richard: Before the parking became a nightmare.

Jessica: The parking is indeed atrocious. It was much easier to get around the old lot.

Ally: It's a maze! And the spots are far too narrow.

Jessica: Way too small. Next to the posts especially! SUVs won't fit. And neither does our Mustang. And what is it with those digital signs?

Rob: I like the new parking lot better because of those digital signs. They show you how many free spaces there are on every level, so you don't have to drive around if a level is full. Yes, there are more spaces crammed in, but it allows 30 per cent more cars to park.

Joseph: But people don't follow signs. They go up the down ramps, and left when they are supposed to go right. I drive at the mall every day and see a lot of dumbass drivers in the parking garage ...

Rob: Joseph, that was me yesterday!

About the Author

David McGee's family moved to Ottawa from Victoria, British Columbia in 1966. He attended Graham Park Public, Bayshore Junior High, Greenbank Junior High, and then Sir Robert Borden High School, where he already displayed his love of history. Graduating with a BA in History from Carleton University, he earned a Ph.D. in the History of Science and Technology from the University of Toronto in 1995, then went off to become a post-doctoral Research Fellow, and later Librarian and Archivist at the Dibner Institute for the History of Science and Technology, located at the Massachusetts Institute of Technology in Cambridge, Massachusetts. McGee returned to Ottawa in 2008 to serve as Librarian  and Archivist for the Canada Science and Technology Museum. There, his role in the acquisition of archival material, particularly the Domtar Eddy Booth Collection, brought him into closer and closer connection with the history of the city. He started Lost Ottawa on Facebook in February of 2013.